jump

Mercy Services

poetry and prose by writerscorps youth

m p

edited by valerie chow bush
introduction by jewelle gomez
photographs by ed kashi

© 2001 WritersCorps Books
Cover art © 2001 Ed Kashi
Introduction © 2001 Jewelle Gomez
Photography © 2001 Ed Kashi
All poems, stories, and art printed with permission
from the authors.

An earlier version of Neil B's poem "The Ghetto"
first appeared in *The Beat Within*, published by
the Pacific News Service.

All rights reserved. No part of this book may be
reproduced or transmitted in any form or by any
means, electronic or mechanical, including photo-
copying or recording, nor may it be introduced into
any information storage and retrieval system without
the written permission of the copyright owner.

ISBN: 1-888048-06-9

WritersCorps Editorial Team:
Valerie Chow Bush, Managing Editor
Janet Heller, WritersCorps Project Manager
Gloria Yamato, WritersCorps Teacher
Mariaynez Carrasco, WritersCorps Student
Russell Reza-Khaliz Gonzaga, Poet and Writer

Thomas Ingalls, Art Director
Sara Streifel, Designer

2000–01 WritersCorps Teachers: Cathy Arellano,
Michelle Matz, Danielle Montgomery, Kimberley
Nelson, Yiskah Rosenfeld, Alison Seevak, Chad
Sweeney, Peter Tamaribuchi, Gloria Yamato.

The San Francisco WritersCorps, a project of the
San Francisco Arts Commission, places writers in
community settings to teach creative writing to
youth. The program is part of a national alliance,
with sites in the Bronx and Washington, D.C., whose
shared vision is to transform and strengthen individ-
uals and communities through the written word.

WritersCorps gratefully acknowledges the support
of the Mayor's Department of Children, Youth and
Their Families; the Department of Juvenile
Probation; the Walter and Elise Haas Fund; the
National Endowment for the Arts; the Richard and
Rhoda Goldman Fund; the Lurie Foundation;
Borders Books and Music; the Gap, Inc.; and
individuals.

For more information, please call 415-252-4655.

www.writerscorps-sf.org

the Contents

Why I Love Aú	**Angelica Pineda**	18
Chinese People Are Not Yellow, They're Peach	**Ivan Cheng**	19
What Makes Me Myself	**Orion Royce Macario**	20
What I See Outside	**Cierra Crowell**	22
Freeway	**Erick McGlothen**	23
My Feelings	**Denise Navarro**	25
On the Playground	**Jen Lindsay's Family Class**	26
The Stone	**Alysha Cornejo**	28
A Bull	**Oscar Leiva**	29
Peace and Magic	**Saman Minapara**	32
Ode to the Bread We Made in Class	**Tawnya Dudash's Grains Class**	33
Map of the Outside	**Charnell Baker**	34
If I Could	**Brandi Barrera**	35
Tea Party under the Sea	**Grace Sizelove**	36
Not Enough Time	**Alice Kwok**	37
My Face	**Seth Gossage**	38
Celebrating Kwanzaa	**Kentoya Ginn**	40
My TV	**Ricky Haro**	41
Who I Am	**Veronica Rodriguez**	43
My Dad, the One I Love	**Prashante Bailey**	44
Getting to Know Me	**Jacqueline Beck**	45
What's Inside the Box	**Fetauo Dunson**	46
The Magic Stone	**Tommy Nguyen**	47
The Daydream	**Hayley Cabrera**	48

Hop

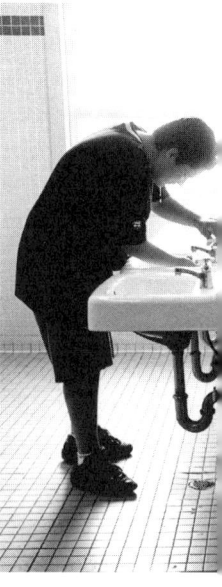

50	The Paper Underneath This Poem	**June Dayao's Class**
51	There Are Animals in Me That Are in My Life	**Athena Mendoza**
52	Elements	**Lily Nguyen**
52	if a tree could talk it would say	**Crystal Doughty**
55	What's Inside Me	**Thalia Marrotin**
56	My Life in the South Pole	**Jonah Varon**
57	Your Heart	**Lena Zheng**
58	The Other Side	**Kali Shelton**
60	Wishes on a Full Stomach	**The Lunch Club**

Skip

62	The Pencil	**Lee Darby**
63	Ode to the Dictionary	**Zhuo Heng Yang**
65	In the Details	**David Mui**
66	Magic Partners	**John Recinos**
67	If I Was a Drought	**Brian Thompson**
68	The House of Peace	**Donald Murphy**
70	Beautiful and Black	**Pauleshia Pulliam**
71	Dear Payless Shoes	**Francisco Quevedo**
73	Ode to Sunset	**Rosa Alvarado**
74	Colors	**Genesis Flota**
75	I'm Sorry	**Lafayette Reed**
77	In the Mind	**Yvette Martinez**
78	Blue	**Angela Phommahaxay**
79	One Less Part	**Jeffrey Lainez**
79	Ode to My Pit Bull	**Valentino Mendoza**
80	Magical Eraser	**Vanessa Borrero**
82	Nature	**Whitney Spencer**
83	La Escuela de Banderas y Puentes	**Jessica Delgado**
83	The School of Flags and Bridges	**Jessica Delgado**

Anthem to the Tree of Freedom   **Qiana Powell**   84
The Kitchen   **Sandy Lam**   85
Inside   **Terry Yan**   87
The Wind   **Anthony Mejia**   88
Two Views of San Francisco   **Johnny Herrera**   89
My Mom Was Born in Guatemala   **Ana Rodriguez**   90
Rain   **Yvette Desantiago**   91
Angel from Above   **Angelica Ochoa**   92
Snowfall over San Francisco   **Linda Nguyen**   94
Rat Boy   **Mastan Sheik**   95
Air   **Jermaine LeBrane**   96
Seeing Myself   **Rosy Mena**   99
Hunger and Beauty   **Tung Nguyen**   100
City Life   **Elizabeth Thompson**   101
My Body   **Gruber Tsang**   103
Rainy Days at School   **Chris McMahon**   104
My Sad Story   **Anaia Gilliam**   105
This Crazy City   **Shahid Minapara**   106

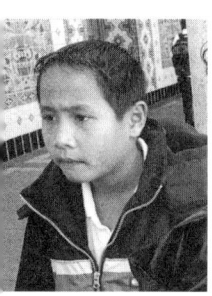

The Fourth of July   **John E. Sweeney**   109
Study Harder   **Cherry Huang**   110
Are You Indian?   **Sadaf Minapara**   111
The Ghetto   **Neil B.**   112
Yellow   **Cherry Mae Brown**   113
I Remember   **Ignacio Sandoval**   114
Addiction   **John E. Sweeney**   116
Pizza   **Dolly Sithounnolat**   117
Bobby   **Neil B.**   118

Jump

120	My Feelings	**Evelyn Morales**
122	How to Be a Little Sister	**Inna Stukova**
123	Shy	**Chia Ling Peng**
124	Tai Shang	**Da Cheng Li**
126	Mental Torment	**Jackie Cabrera**
127	Urban Life	**Andrew E.**
128	Ode to My Sister Zulma	**Karen Valenzuela**
129	My Father	**Craig F.**
132	Poetry	**Asefa Subedar**
134	Questions for the Great Wall	**Cathy She**
135	The Right Side of Upside Down	**DeAngelo R.**
136	Pomegranate	**Song Zhao Gong**
137	Tulips	**Ricky Hernandez**
139	Me	**LiLi Liang**
140	My Chrysanthemum Tea	**Kristy Ruan**
141	Grandmom	**Christy Allen**
141	Poetry	**Roger Duan**
143	Okra	**Angelo Richardson**
144	Grandma	**Janie Fung**
145	The Crush	**Vanessa Soriano**
146	In My Past Life	**Cindy Wu**

Leap

148	What Poetry Should Be	**Anwar Collins**
150	Are You Doing That New Drug Thing?	**Michael Currie**
151	Take It Back	**Angelo Phillips**
153	Regret	**Everick S.**

Ain't Nobody Understands Me **Daniel A.** 154
Indian Spirit **Octavio S.** 157
Haiku **Ignacio Sanchez** 158
Haiku **Karen Au** 158
Abandoned **Daniel A.** 159
A Poem for the Man **Marlene Sanchez** 160
Hell of Angels **Robert C.** 161
One and Only **Anastasia** 162
Our Year **Jessica Nowlan-Green** 164
Praise the Blue-Collared **Raoul Tom** 165
Love Poem for Home **Jessica Nowlan-Green** 167
Family Night Out **Daniel A.** 168

When I Forget Why I Teach **Alison Seevak** 170
Breaking Ground **Yiskah Rosenfeld** 172
why i teach writing **Danielle Montgomery** 174
Whatever Gets You Through the Night or Hot Manju **Peter Tamaribuchi** 176
Mission Girls **Cathy Arellano** 178
Trying to Be Men **Kimberley Nelson** 182
The Arc of Intention **Chad Sweeney** 184
Libation for the Present and Future **Gloria Yamato** 186
Make Room **Michelle Matz** 187

Soar
Teachers' Writings

foreword

I have had the honor of being associated with WritersCorps since its inception in 1994. Over the past seven years, the San Francisco Arts Commission has proudly administered the program. How different—and more glorious—the community arts landscape looks now than it did in those early years when WritersCorps was one of the few arts-based service programs in the nation.

I am so inspired to see, on a daily basis, how WritersCorps changes lives. Whether teachers are working with youth in juvenile detention, recent immigrants grappling with a new language, or single teen mothers, their impact is profound. Observing WritersCorps in action, I marvel at the power the written and spoken word can have on our sense of self and of our place in the world.

WritersCorps reminds me why I love my work. As I read poems from a site's chapbook, watch youth compete at the poetry slams, or listen to them read from each year's anthology, I see the lasting effects WritersCorps has on all those it touches. I thank each student, teacher, parent, and staff member for making WritersCorps part of my life.

This year's anthology, *Jump*, is funny, sad, moving, and beautiful. Each piece of writing gives us a glimpse into a life full of promise, anticipation, and hope for the future. I urge you to read the work of these young writers, and to allow them to move you as they have moved me.

Rich Newirth
Director of Cultural Affairs
San Francisco Arts Commission

introduction

When I was a kid I loved to jump rope. I thrilled to the rhythm of the girls keeping count with the clever story rhymes passed down through the generations. At the same time, their firm swinging kept the double-Dutch ropes from tangling. The sound of feet skipping in counterpoint to singsong ditties and ropes tapping on the urban pavement was like a heartbeat to me, signaling both the simplicities and the complications of being a child in the city. As we jumped, we were carrying on a tradition that embodied both our physical prowess and our mental agility.

Later, I lived in an apartment overlooking a schoolyard, and every day I listened to the high-pitched squeals of encouragement as girls and boys egged each other on to make higher scores. Whether they were jumping rope or going up for a jump ball under the basket, their enthusiasm was infectious. These games of perpetual motion seemed like perfect metaphors for the heart of a healthy, youthful life: undaunted movement toward joy and growth.

The first time I read a poem, I loved it because it reminded me of those simple jump-rope rhymes and the excitement of leaping into the air. That poem (whose title I've long forgotten) was telling a story and telling me how powerful my feelings could be. The energy a string of well-considered words can create is as thrilling as any jump I've ever made.

The work of the young writers in *Jump* creates the same rush of exhilaration. Their poetry and prose is bursting with energy on the page, whatever the form— free-style, haiku, hip-hop, or epic—or the topic. One student articulates sophisticated impatience with stereotypes about her Indian heritage, another identifies the magic of a blank piece of paper, and another remembers the tastes and sounds of Guacamayas. A student assures us that her "fears are kept in boxes in the basement/and no one can know about them." Reading those words, I feel that her ability to locate those fears and announce them in print may be the most important step toward banishing them. Each of these poems opens new worlds to us, sometimes familiar and occasionally uncomfortable.

The values of a program such as WritersCorps are multilayered. The skilled and enthusiastic WritersCorps artists who share with their students the passion and practicalities of writing are preparing the way for the next literary generation. They can teach young people the emotional and intellectual equivalent of jumping rope. By writing, students learn that their lives are worthy of observation and discussion, worthy of their own attention even if others—parents, teachers, other adults—fail them. They can begin to tell the stories of their lives with rhythm and style, perseverance and stamina. And this can give them the skills to keep moving in a life that often puts obstacles in their paths.

The voices of young people on a playground or reading their poems out loud is one of the most hopeful sounds any of us will ever hear. The giggles and shouts, the shy intonations let us know there is still a future worth believing in. When a young poet writes, "I am the light in your room," she confirms that belief.

The poems in this collection all tell us to jump in—the water is just fine.

Jewelle Gomez

Jewelle Gomez, author of *The Gilda Stories*, is the new director of the Cultural Equity Grants Program of the San Francisco Arts Commission.

one Hop

Why I Love Aú

When I do aú
I feel like I am flying
and as I fly I grin.

When I do aú
I feel like a bird in the air
and as I fly in the air I sing a sweet tweet.

I spin and grin
and it makes me
feel the wind.

When I sing the music
I feel the movement.

When I get dizzy and tired
my teacher says,
"Come on, guys, let's be admired!"

I don't give up because I love aús.
Aús can be blue, but I love it.
Put power in yourself.

Angelica Pineda, 8
Girls After School Academy

Aú is a move in the popular Brazilian martial art of capoeira that closely resembles a cartwheel.

Chinese People Are Not Yellow, They're Peach

I'm a Chinese boy.
I was peach but now I'm burned peach
because I am always in the sun.
First I was little and then I was big
but burned peach is just the same as peach.
It doesn't matter what color
your skin is.

Ivan Cheng, 8
San Francisco Community School

What Makes Me Myself

I come from math because every part of my body
is a fraction, a decimal, and a percentage.
My mathematics knowledge makes me myself.

The color blue is the color of sky, the color of the ocean.
My favorite color is the color of myself.

Pizza—ah, pizza—is one of the foods that make me myself.
I have a lot of friends, like the toppings on a pizza.

Superman is my kind of superhero.
He can fly high, he can fly low, he can fly fast, he can fly slow.
He is as strong as an ox. I want to be Superman and fly,
or a karate master who punches and kicks really fast.

The violin's sound is a rhythm in my heart that heals my wounds.

I am safe in my bedroom because it is a really private place.
Mexico is the place I would rather be instead of San Francisco.

I am the yin and yang of the Chinese symbol.

Sweetheart is the one name you should not call me
or you will feel deep pain.

Speaking five languages makes me more sociable.

I love swimming in the summer, in the river, in the lake,
with the fish, being like the fish.
I am happy as a dog wagging my tail.

I am the moon in the night sky.
I am the sky where my friends,
the moon and the stars, hang from.

                                              Orion Royce Macario, 11
                                              San Francisco Community School

Everett Middle School

What I See Outside

I see a bunch of flowers
staring at me, wondering if I
will pick them or leave them
where they belong. I see a fountain
with a cruel face and, across the street, a school
where children come to learn and play.
Sitting beside me are flower-bells hanging.
Behind me are plants with sun and shadow,
both reflecting at the same time,
and beneath is dark soil sucking water for the plants.
I also see trees with leaves like
cocoons hanging on a branch,
and the spiky leaves of palm trees.
Now people are walking home from work.

Across the street, I see a group of people
working together, making new apartments.
The big crane looks like a scorpion
holding its tail over its head.
On top of the building, the American flag
is waving back and forth.

I see clouds that look like ocean shores
with waves smashing on the clouds.

When I look up, I see tops of buildings
and birds flying over the tops of trees
and different kinds of flags.

When I look down, I see cracks and bugs.

That's what I see when I look out,
look up, look down
and look in front of me.

Cierra Crowell, 8
Mercy Services

Freeway

I am the freeway.
I hear lots of cars.
I smell candy bars.

I feel kind of mad
because the cars won't stop riding over me.

I have a cousin
who's very far away.
His name is the Golden Gate Bridge
and that's what I say.

Erick McGlothen, 8
San Francisco Community School

YWCA Mission Girls Services

My Feelings

Inside me is a sun,
shining and shining on everyone.
Inside me is a bird, flying and soaring.
Inside me is a snake.
It makes me mad and it rattles
to let you know when you're too close.
Inside me is a tree, tall and shady.
Inside me is a dying flower.
I get sadder and sadder.
Inside me is the sky.
I hold it inside.
I won't let thunder roar.

Inside me is a heart that is dancing.

Denise Navarro, 8
San Francisco Community School

On the Playground

On the playground
I see a bus, yellow as mustard,
yellow like my jacket.
I see a big gate.
I see the playing structure.
It looks like a monster,
the left hand a slide,
the right hand spinning.

When I close my eyes, I hear a jackhammer
that sounds like a monkey jumping up and down.
I hear a plane that sounds like a hurricane.
I hear a flag standing strong and proud.
I hear jumping that sounds like bricks
falling on each other.
I hear a car zooming by like a dryer.
I hear my heart beating like a drum.

I feel a rose, spiky and soft.
I feel a log and it gives me splinters.
Grass and hay and dirt together feel hard.
I feel the dirt and it's smooth.
I feel big.

When I look up, I get dizzy.
I see an airplane flying through the sky,
and it looks like it is swimming.
I feel like I am falling from the sky.
I feel like I am getting hypnotized.
I feel tall.

When I close my eyes,
I see red spots,
I see Batman,
I see my heart beating fast.

When I look really close,
I find an ant that looks like three little spots.
I take a little dot of dirt
and touch grass like spikes and green as a dinosaur.
I see a rock as little as a crumb.

Jen Lindsay's Family Class, 8 to 9
San Francisco Community School

Mercy Services

The Stone

        The   pink
  stone looks   like a heart.
It is as pink as a painted teardrop.
It is as pink as the sky when the sun's
  coming down. When you give your
     mom or dad a Valentine,
        it is like this
          stone.

Alysha Cornejo, 8
San Francisco Community School

A Bull

A bull snaps when it sees red.
It goes wild.
It attacks whoever gets in its way.
It is even capable of injuring anybody.
It has a hot temper.
A bull is dangerous.
A bull is big and strong,
and it is not ashamed of the country it comes from.
A bull is full of pride.
A bull represents me,
Oscar Antonio Leiva.

Oscar Leiva, 11
San Francisco Community School

Peace and Magic

I.

I hear peace all around me.
The wind,
the trees blowing,
rain dropping, the flowers
bending.

I hear the lights flashing,
birds pecking,
and footsteps walking.

I hear window blinds closing,
the grass growing,
and flowers blooming.

II.

With my magic I can
grab tiny rocks from the bottom of the pond
and pull a cloud from the sky.
I can build a big skyscraper
and eat a bag of chips
or catch a butterfly.

I can shoot an arrow at the moon
and sun.

Saman Minapara, 8
Mercy Services

Ode to the Bread We Made in Class

My bread looks brown and crunchy,
like a rock with pieces breaking off.
From the top,
it could be a flower opening up.
At the bottom,
it feels like a sponge.

My bread looks like a big balloon with purple spots on it.
It looks like a light-brown, fluffy chocolate-chip cookie.
It looks like the tip of a spaceship.
It looks like a couch or maybe a beanbag chair.
It's shaped like the moon
or a heart
or a footrest.

When I tap it,
it sounds like a drum.
When I break off a piece,
it sounds like a peanut breaking off the shell,
it sounds like an ant is eating it,
it sounds like a tiny, tiny, tiny, tiny heart beating.

When I finally bite it with my two front teeth
it's like eating something soft, like a pillow.
It tastes sweet and sour.
It tastes like Mother Nature's hair.
It tastes warm like a blanket in bed.

Tawnya Dudash's Grains Project Class, 8 to 10
San Francisco Community School

Map of the Outside

Flowers
smooth
bees
buzzing
screaming and yelling
dripping water
cars
and a big school.

I see a gate with diamonds
the color of a dolphin
and I eat purple green
it smells like Listerine
the wind tapping in my ear
and haystacks
brown and black.

Charnell Baker, 8
San Francisco Community School

If I Could   I'd be
the person who
does not like to wake up
in the morning.

I'd be
the person who
does not want to sleep at night.

I'd be
myself
to live the life
that I am supposed to live.

Brandi Barrera, 10
San Francisco Community School

Tea Party under the Sea

Under the sea there are houses
for mermaids
and schools for fish.
I invite everyone over for tea.
Everyone comes—they always do.

I need big tables, small tables, and medium tables.
They are very messy eaters.

First, there's the Loch Ness monster,
and the whales,
the big fish.

The mediums are the mermaids and eels.

The small fish are in schools
that come on field trips.

We have themes every time we have a tea party.
This time it is a '50s theme,
so everyone wears their fake hairdos
and leather jackets,
and we dance to Elvis and watch *Grease*.

I wonder what will happen next time.

Grace Sizelove, 10
Mercy Services

Not Enough Time

I am a busy young girl.
I never ever have time for
things I really want to do.

I am someone
who cannot see my own reflection.
I always do things my way.

I wish I really had time
to sit on the beach,
feel the wind and hear
the beautiful waves
coming back and forth.

Alice Kwok, 11
San Francisco Community School

My Face

My eyes are like a planet cut in half, showing the core.
My nose is a vacuum that sucks in air and pushes it out.
My cheeks are like cushions.
My eyebrows are strips of grass growing over my eyes.
My hair is like the tops of trees.
My teeth are big mashing machines.
My mouth is a wing flapping up and down.
My ears are like big valleys.
My eyelids are like shades.
My eyelashes are barriers catching things
that fall from above.

Seth Gossage, 10
San Francisco Community School

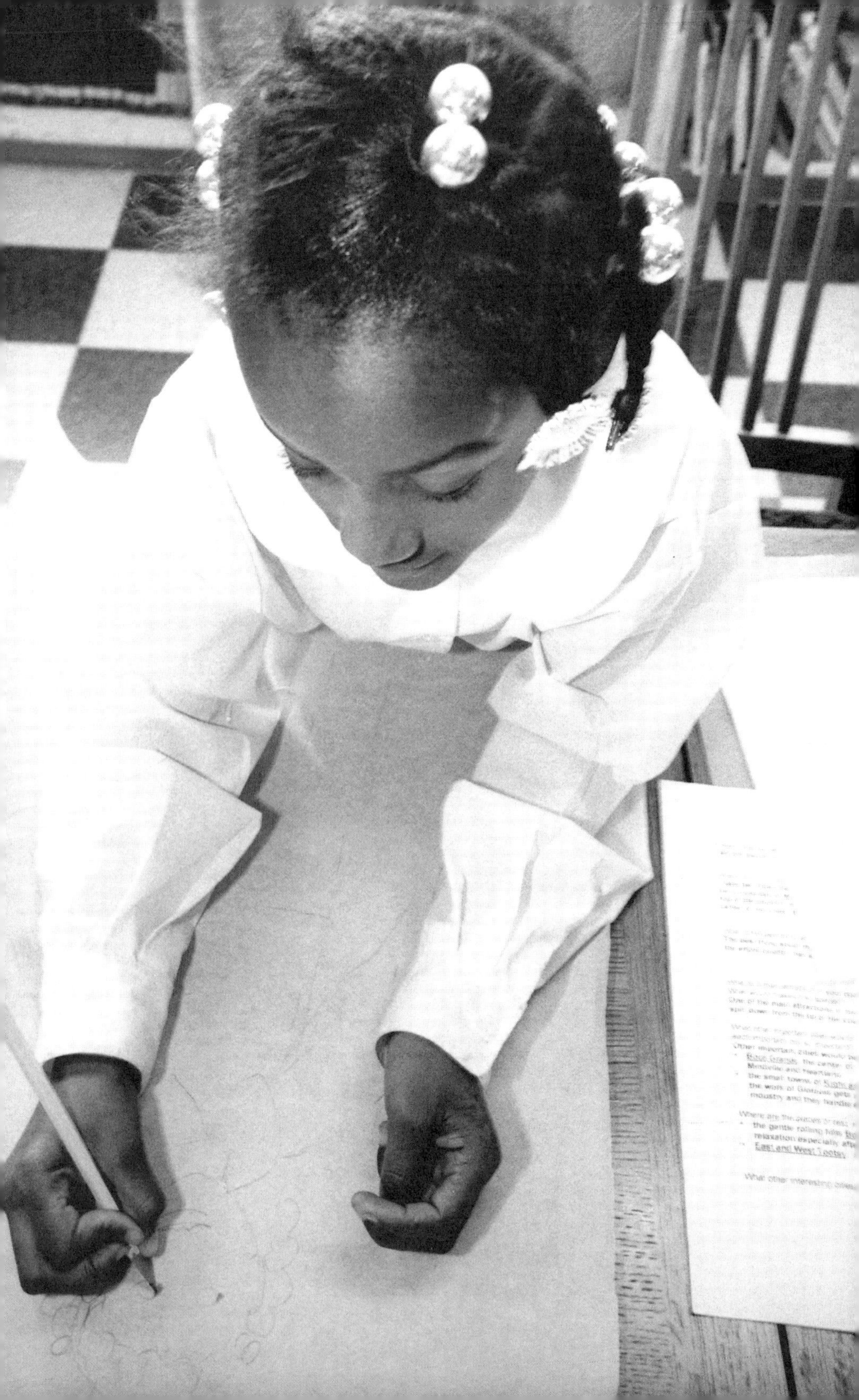

Celebrating Kwanzaa

I like when we're
all singing and dancing.

We have very loud voices.
We hear all kinds of sounds

like clapping, stomping our feet,
drums, birimbau, cowbells

and stuff like that.
We sing capoeira songs.

We do hip-hop dancing,
like the leg pop and the tick tock

you know
stuff like that.

                      Kentoya Ginn, 10
                      Girls After School Academy

My TV

My TV said, "Never get cable!"

My TV is color-blind,
and when he laughs, the volume
goes higher.

When I change the channel, he changes
language and attitude.
And when he's off, he rests
for the day.

Ricky Haro, 10
Mercy Services

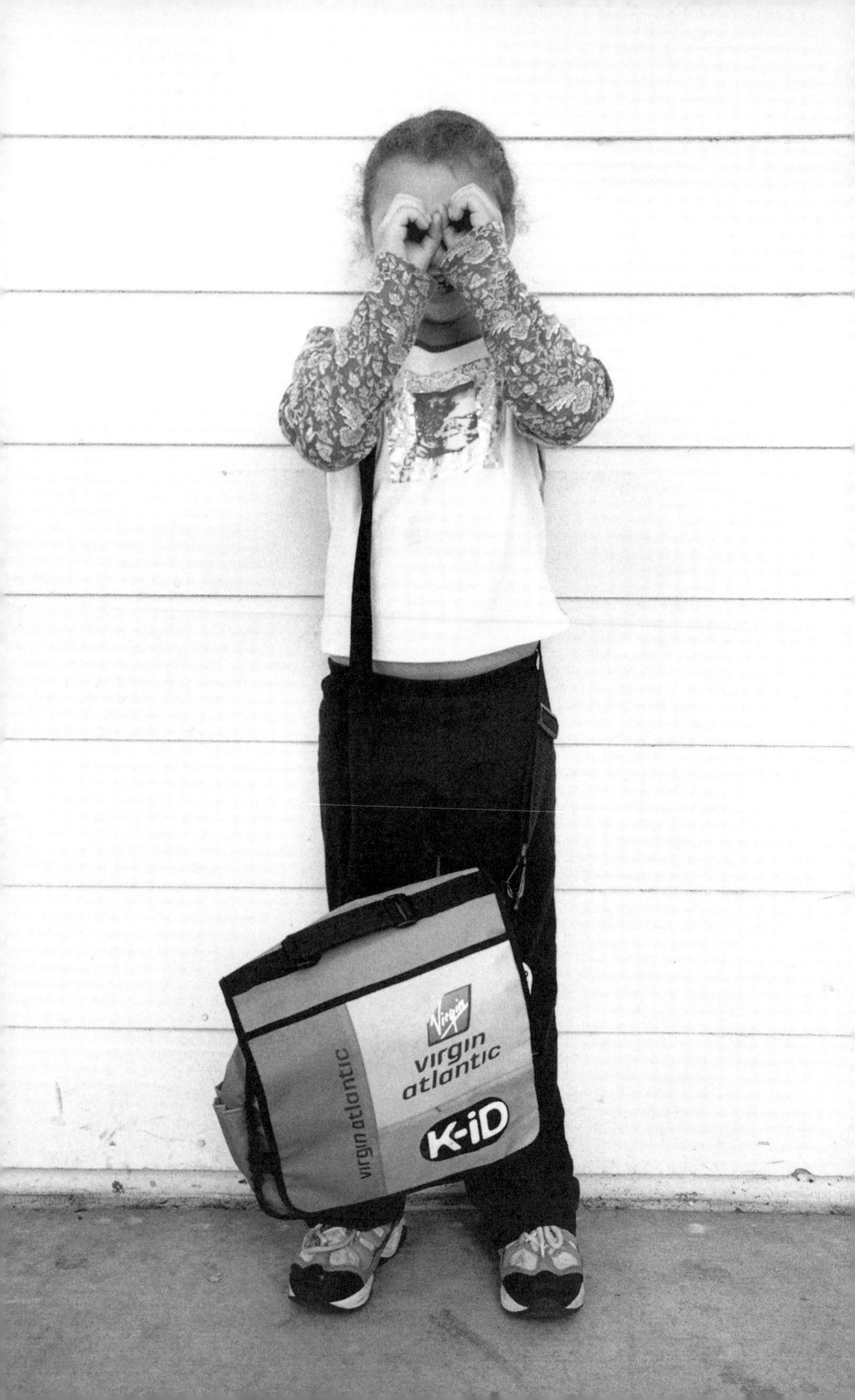
Virgin
virgin atlantic
virgin atlantic
K-iD

Who I Am

I am the best singer that ever lived.
When I sing, people forget their problems.

I am a great basketball player,
and I can beat anyone at it.

I am a cloud floating
in the beautiful sky.

I am an angel and I can fly
anywhere I want to fly.

But really I'm just a sixth-grade girl
named Veronica Rodriguez.
And I'm proud of it.

                    Veronica Rodriguez, 11
                    San Francisco Community School

My Dad, the One I Love

My dad is gone for a few days.
I made my dad a book
to tell me what's happening when he is gone.
He's going to tell me what's going on in Florida.

Dad, on the airplane wish for me,
but come back for my brother
and back for my birthday
and come back for me.

Prashante Bailey, 9
San Francisco Community School

Getting to Know Me

My thoughts are birds
soaring through the sky.
Night and day, my teeth take baths
with giant toothbrushes.

My fingers are clusters
of bananas, and my toes
wiggle
like piano keys playing.

My eyebrows are worms
getting warm and lying down.
My mouth
opens wide like the closet.

Jacqueline Beck, 12
Mercy Services

What's Inside the Box

A snake hissing
A gorilla roaring
Earrings that sound like bells
Broken glass
Pencils rockin' to the beat
My sister snoring
Rocks falling from cliffs
Dropping combs from the sky
Storm crashing into houses
The sun making the windows crack
A lion scratching behind his ears
My sister burping
My brother stomping his feet
People walking down the halls
People wetting their hair
and flipping it back
Pennies falling on the floor
Me stomping at cockroaches
Ketchup squirting from the bottle
Water rushing through the rocks
That's what I think's in the box.

What about you?

Fetauo Dunson, 9
San Francisco Community School

The Magic Stone

One day a dragon
had to go find a golden stone
to help his people.

Looking for the stone, he found
a snake.
The snake wanted to help him find the stone,
so the dragon agreed.

They worked and looked and worked and looked,
until they found
a funny monkey.
The monkey wanted to join them,
so the dragon and the snake agreed.

The new friends worked and looked and worked and looked,
until they found
the enemy!
The enemy found the stone first and flew
up to his sky city in the clouds.

The group of friends traveled up to the city.
They hid from the guard and snuck into the castle.
They captured the golden stone and returned home.
The dragon was the hero of his people.

The End. (All good fairy tales have to say this!)

Tommy Nguyen, 9
Mercy Services

The Daydream

When I look up at the sky,
I see a blue cloud. It turns into shapes.
It looks like a dolphin, then it looks like a cherry.
When I lie down in the green soft grass, I see a grasshopper.
I imagine the grasshopper is a heart with some legs.
It is pretty like my mom.

I wish I was a pillow
because I could smell the sweet smell of the person's shampoo.
Then I wish I was a rainbow because at the end of my rainbow feet
could be a pot of gold or a pot of Skittles.
But then I want to be a flower because the wind will blow
and my petals, which are my hair, will blow away.
Then I can feel the wind blowing on my head.

        Hayley Cabrera, 8
        San Francisco Community School

YWCA Mission Girls Services

The Paper Underneath This Poem

Paper is white
like the shades
or a ghost
or bubbles
or a polar bear
or brand-new sneakers
or the face
of a clock.

Paper is flat
like a kite
or tissues.

Paper can be as sharp
as a butcher knife
or as smooth as a table.
As sharp as scissors
or as smooth as glass.
As sharp as a pen
or as smooth as water.
As sharp as fangs
or as smooth as dolphins
and fine sand.

Paper sounds like
garbage
fire
popcorn
horseshoes
static on the radio
shaking maracas.

Paper sounds like rain.

June Dayao's Class, 8 to 11
San Francisco Community School

There Are Animals in Me
That Are in My Life

There's a cat in me,
he makes me mad.

There's a German shepherd in me
that gives me power
to run fast speeds.

There's an Alaskan malamute
that makes me wild.

There's a hamster in me,
he makes me feel like I'm in a cage.

There's a rabbit in me
that makes me sniff.

There's an ox in me
that makes me eat a lot.

There's a butterfly
that makes me feel good.

There's a chicken
that makes me talk a lot.

There's an owl in me
that makes me ask too many questions.

There's a guinea pig
that makes me calm.

There's a chick in me
that makes me feel cute.

Athena Mendoza, 10
YWCA Mission Girls Services

Elements

Earth is the feeling of green
soft grass in the spring,
the touch of a bird's
light-brown feather.

Fire makes you want to burn
your finger
black as burnt apple. It's the liquid
of a jeweler melting
a bar of shiny gold,
the fever of a dangerous
beast of the jungle.

Rain is the eye
of the wind blowing,
the sound of tsunami
in the clear ocean,
sound of a whispering friend.

Lily Nguyen, 11
Mercy Services

if a tree could talk it would say

crystal, will you be
my best friend?

i like you!

my name is jennifer.

will you scratch my
arm, please,
because i'm itchy?

ouch! get down from me!

Crystal Doughty, 5
Mercy Services

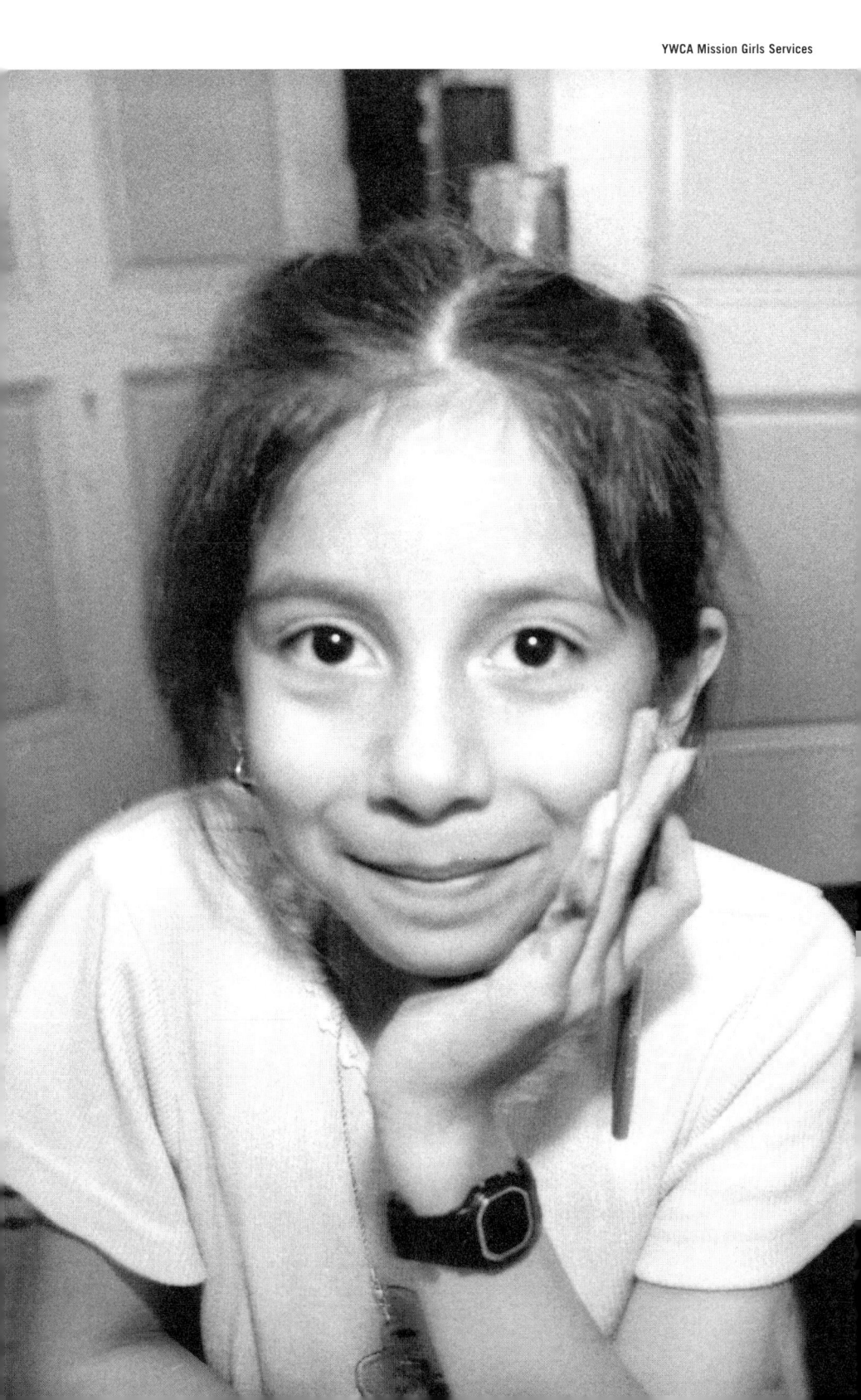

YWCA Mission Girls Services

Everett Middle School

What's Inside Me

There is a cheetah inside me,
it gives me the power of speed.
There is a rabbit in me,
it gives me the power to go.
There is a butterfly in me,
it gives me the power to be beautiful.

Thalia Marrotin, 6
YWCA Mission Girls Services

My Life in the South Pole

My name is Jonah Levy Varon.
I live underground, in the South Pole.
When you hear noise inside my house, don't panic.
It's just my restless unicorns rampaging around the living room.
When I'm hungry, I hunt mammoths.
Life is white.
In the summer, the sun never sets.
It looks like a fiery ball, suspended by a string as thin as dental floss.
Where the snow melts, it turns into streams.
I go sledding, skiing, and snowboarding.

For my holidays, I visit Hawaii.
There is a house inside a volcano that I often stay in.

Jonah Varon, 9
San Francisco Community School

Your Heart

Your heart should shine,
your heart is a gold mine.
You're the only one
who can dig through it.
There's a very large pit
to your deepest, darkest secret.

Lena Zheng, 10
San Francisco Community School

The Other Side

When you look out at the freeway,
you might see cars,
but I see rainbow lights
scattering this way and that.

When you look out at the city,
you might see buildings and houses,
but I see a magical and peaceful place.

When you look out your window,
you might see a dirty bus,
but I see toys
dancing off the walls and seats.

                Kali Shelton, 11
                San Francisco Community School

Mercy Services

Wishes on a Full Stomach

I wish I would grow up faster.
I wish I could shine the gold I have in me.
I wish I had wings to fly around the world.
I wish it would snow and the snow
would turn into a rainbow
then bubble away and wander.
I wish I had a cosmic charm.
I wish I had a nose as long as Pinocchio's so I could smell the flowers.
I wish I lived in a fortress of flame.
I wish every problem would be solved.
I wish I was a blue bird flying over the sea.
I wish I was in fantasy land.
I wish my bed was a soft cloud.
I wish I stayed young forever.
I wish all my wishes would come true.

>The Lunch Club, 8 to 11
>San Francisco Community School

two **Skip**

The Pencil

The pencil nervously
shook
during the Stanford
Nine Test at Everett
because the kid did
not study and
did not
know any of
the answers.
The pencil that first
was big
now is small
from being
sharpened so much.

Lee Darby, 14
Everett Middle School

Ode to the Dictionary

In the world,
in the shops,
dictionaries everywhere.
The dictionary is very great.
It is just like my mother.
If no dictionary,
I wouldn't have a future.
The dictionary
is also like my teacher.
It tells me
a lot of knowledge,
many sentences,
many words,
much poetry,
and a lot of data.
When I feel bored,
I can play games
on the dictionary.
When the dictionary
is just like my teacher,
it tells me
what is past tense,
present perfect,
progressive tense.
When I don't know the word,
it can tell me about this word.

Zhuo Heng Yang, 14
Newcomer High School

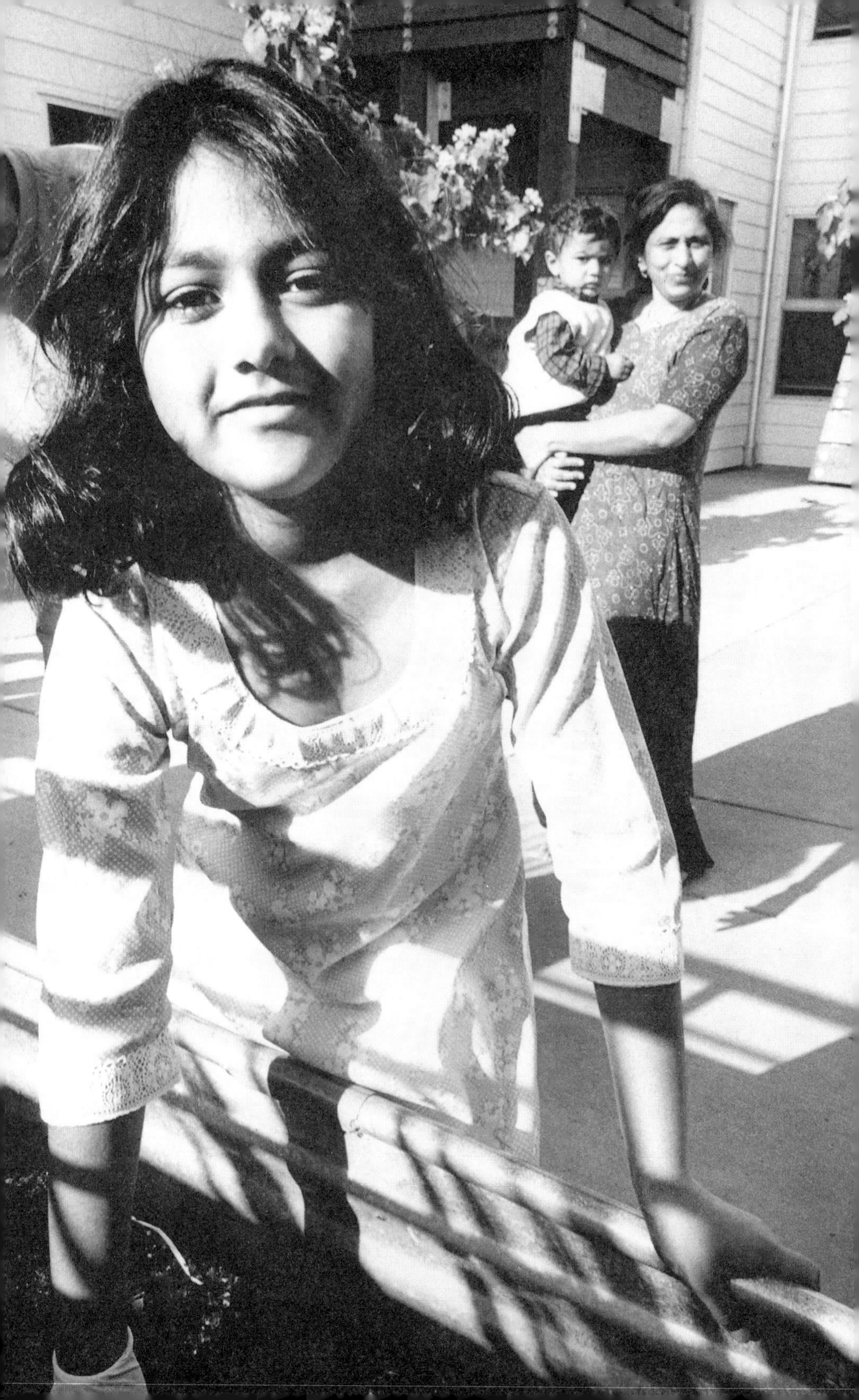

In the Details

Pink flowers
in the tree,
skinny rain gutter,
cracked
tile on the roof,
old broom standing alone,
domed cupola of a church,
power lines,
ivory cross,
half a butterfly
wing.

David Mui, 14
Everett Middle School

Magic Partners

Me and Brian like to do magic tricks,
like guessing colors
or multiplying objects.
We make coins disappear.
My uncle once told me
I should do magic for money.
He also said we should be partners—
I do magic,
he gets the money.

>John Recinos, 12
>Everett Middle School

If I Was a Drought

If I could be a natural disaster
I would be a drought
because they are highly underrated.
A tornado will happen and everyone
will be all, "Oh, no" and "That's so terrible,"
but a drought is no biggie.
Droughts are so ashamed of not being frightening
that they sit in a corner all the time
and only come out when they have to.

Brian Thompson, 12
Everett Middle School

The House of Peace

In the house of peace
there is no need
for fire
because the sun is shining
just for the people.

There's a chair in the house
that talks
and helps God decide
people's fate.
It is green and
pink with mushrooms on it.

The rooms are like mood rings.
If you feel a certain way, the room
will change to the color you feel.

There are windows as clear as can be,
and just by looking at them
they shine more.

> Donald Murphy, 14
> Everett Middle School

Girls After School Academy

Beautiful and Black

Black and beautiful,
yeah, that's me.

Black and beautiful,
that's what you can call me.

Average-type hair,
don't judge me from the things that I wear.

Don't say smart words
because I don't care.

Girl, go and put your hair
in any way you want to wear it.

Well, I'm not the one who can tell you
when and where to do something

because it is your choice.

I am black and beautiful
because that's what I want to be called.

Don't call me names behind a thick-ass wall.
Girl, come tell me,

we can talk
and work it out.

Pauleshia Pulliam, 13
Girls After School Academy

Dear Payless Shoes

Dear Payless Shoes,

So long!
We don't want to see your cheap shoes anymore.
Once you put them on,
they turn wrinkly, dirty,
and begin to fall apart.
Once someone puts on your shoes
and runs,
Rip!
There go those shoes.

Francisco Quevedo, 12
Everett Middle School

Girls After School Academy

Ode to Sunset

First of amber, melt the sky,
what was blue has now turned pink.
Shore, the pink with the sea below,
silk so smooth it makes you cry,
reflects the light that's sent below.
Darts of heat pierce my skin,
reach the cave that I call heart.
See that no one lives in there,
ignite a flame of wild red,
first of ruby, melt the pain.

Rosa Alvarado, 12
Everett Middle School

Colors

I paint with the colors
of my ancestors' spirits.
Artists sing to me the colors
that I paint with.

Genesis Flota, 13
Everett Middle School

I'm Sorry

I'm sorry.
Sorry that you look the way you do.
Sorry for the pain they put you through.
Sorry that your best friends let you down.
Sorry that you have no one to play with
and you sit there with a frown.
Sorry that I never asked to be your friend.
Sorry that I never tried to see the pain you had within.
Sorry that I overlooked how you feel inside.
Sorry that when they made fun of you,
I wasn't on your side.
Sorry, but I'll be your friend now.
Sorry, but there'll be no more frets or frowns.
Now I'll be your friend, no more pain within.
Now I realize and I apologize.
Sorry.

                        Lafayette Reed, 12
                        San Francisco Community School

Everett Middle School

In the Mind

My fears are kept
in boxes in the basement,
and no one can know about them
except me.
My feelings are kept in the attic,
locked up,
so no one can hurt them or know about them.
Some windows are clean and some dirty,
so my mind can see what it wants to see.

There is a long stairway that never
ends, and not even I
can understand.

There is only one clock,
the Clock of Life,
and I don't know when it will stop.

In my mind there are solid doors
that look like a big maze
going on forever.
I don't have a key to all the doors.
I wonder when I will have the keys
and can open them all up.

Yvette Martinez, 13
Everett Middle School

Blue

When blue comes to me I think of the sky,
how clouds are floating sadly or happily.
Blue.

When I think of the color blue I think of gangs,
how my brother is in one.
Every minute, hour, and day that passes by
I wonder if he's going to get hurt.

When I think of blue I think of sadness,
how I never got to see or know my grandparents,
how I had a chance to see them when they were alive,
but I didn't take it.

Is blue just a color to you?

Blue makes me think of the ocean and the fish,
how they are trying to hide in the clear blue water.

Blue.
It's not only sadness,
or is it?
When I say, "I feel blue,"
what do I mean?

Does blue mean something to you?

Angela Phommahaxay, 12
Everett Middle School

One Less Part

I am a clown without a smile.
I am an angel without a wing.
I am a clock without hands.
I am a hat without a top.

Jeffrey Lainez, 12
Everett Middle School

Ode to My Pit Bull

My pit bull has white spots and brown fur.
He sounds like a squeaky door when he barks.
My pit bull feels like a porcupine.
He smells like raspberries.
My pit bull fights like Hector Macho Camacho
when he's aggressive.

Valentino Mendoza, 13
Everett Middle School

Magical Eraser

She wouldn't believe this pencil has
a magical eraser.
She said I was silly.
She said I was a liar, too.
She dared me to prove that it was true,
and so what could I do?

I erased her.

Vanessa Borrero, 12
Everett Middle School

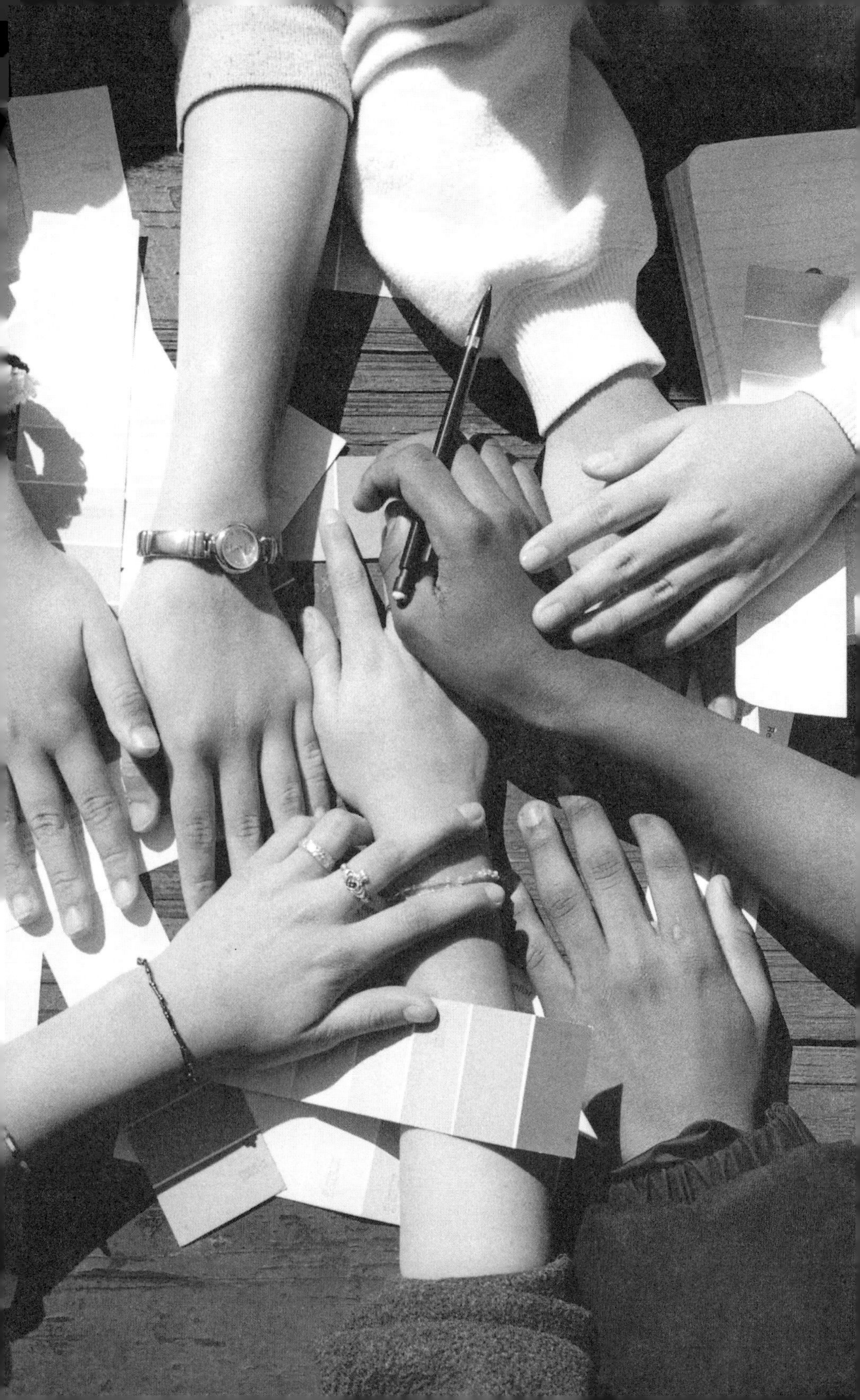

Nature

Crackling wood makes me think of camping,
the sound of fireflies buzzing over the trees,
of wind rustling over the dry leaves
and making them scratch the dirt,
watching the moon and stars fall over you
like a blanket,
and morning wrapping around you
like hot cocoa with marshmallows.

Whitney Spencer, 13
Everett Middle School

La Escuela de Banderas y Puentes

Mi escuela es hecha de calles,
y ropa tendida,
tejas y piso.

En mi escuela se ve el cielo
y pájaros
sobre montañas.

Mi escuela es mi casa.
Es la iglesia. Es ventanas y cables.

Mi escuela es una manguera,
palmas, cortinas.

Es personas y águilas,
banderas y puentes.

Mi escuela es jardines y viento.

The School of Flags and Bridges

My school is made of streets,
and clothes drying on the line,
roofs and floor.

In my school one sees sky
and birds
over mountains.

My school is my house.
It is church. It is windows and cables.

My school is a garden hose,
palm trees, curtains.

It is people and eagles,
flags and bridges.

My school is gardens and wind.

Jessica Delgado, 13
Everett Middle School

Anthem to the Tree of Freedom

From a seed to a strong, mighty tree,
there stands the Tree of Freedom.
From Martin Luther King's
"I have a dream!"
to Rosa Parks fighting
for the front of that bus,
we will forever stand with no fear inside
because God shall be with us!

The tears we've shed day and night,
the words we've prayed to keep our faith,
the lives that were taken shall not rest in peace.
The hopes that have fallen pick us up,
and we believed,
we believed this seed
would grow to freedom!

Indeed, yes! We will forever stand, no fear inside
because God shall be with us.
Those who have died shall still remain here inside
because of their mighty pride.

Indeed, yes! We shall overcome someday.
We shall walk hand in hand,
no more sorrow in our hearts.
We shall forever stand,
saying, "That path was dark, but now I'm free!"
No more chains will remain.
No more people getting hanged.
No more sacks on our backs.
No more suffering through pain.
No more sisters getting raped.
No more picking cotton in the rain.
No more lives being taken.
All our lives will change!

Because of our faith,
because we believed that the seed
would grow to freedom and forever stand,
the Tree of Freedom!

Qiana Powell, 14
Everett Middle School

The Kitchen

The can of soup
wonders when I am finally going
to empty it out into the saucepan, heat it up,
and eat it.

The knife wants to cut the fork in half.

The cookie jar wonders why I am lying
to my mother about who ate the cookies.

The stove wants me to take it camping
so it can cook for me outdoors.

The garbage disposal decides not to work.

The sink wonders why I always talk to it
when I'm really thinking out loud.

Sandy Lam, 13
Everett Middle School

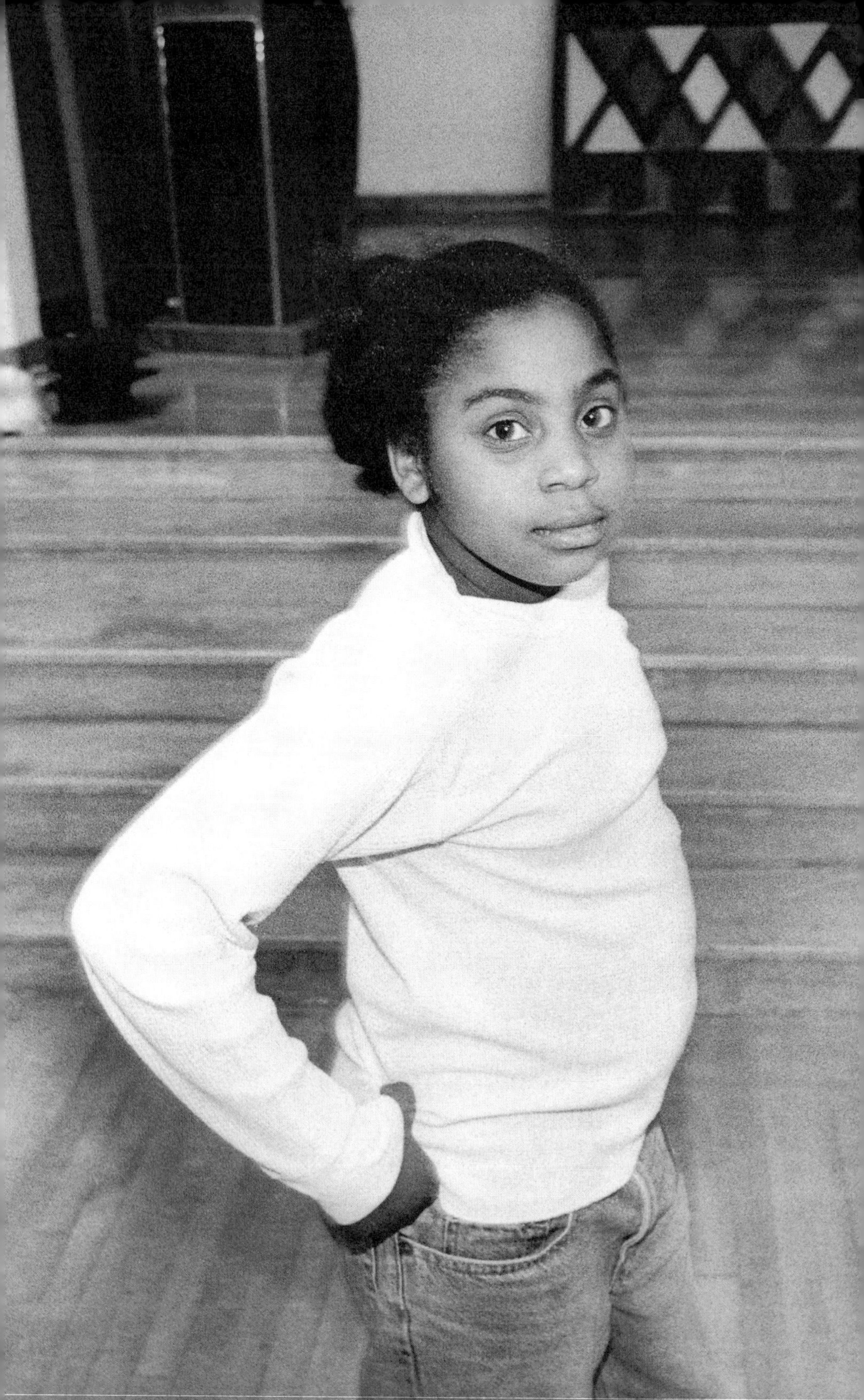

Inside

Inside me
are stairs
that lead to many bright rooms.

One room is blue with blue roses.

Another has a tiger running through a forest.
One room has a wall made entirely of a clock.
Another is filled with movies that flood my thoughts.

In the attic is a waterfall
dropping through the dark sky
as rain.

Music roams down the halls.

A room of caves holds my anger
with blinding light to hurt
your eye.

Terry Yan, 13
Everett Middle School

The Wind

I am the wind
that blows your window curtains
apart, the wind that blows the leaves
off the trees and onto the dry grass.

I am that wind!

I can be gentle
or mad, but no matter what,
I am still that wind.
When I am gentle, I blow
not even an ant,
but when I'm mad, I shatter everything.

I am the wind!

I can mix
with water
to become hurricane
and after, nothing but rain.
I am the rain
going away
as the summer comes.

But I'll be back.
I will be born from rivers, lakes, and oceans.
I am that rain.

        Anthony Mejia, 13
        Everett Middle School

Two Views of San Francisco

I.

I see buildings,
people come in and out of every day,
murals of life that give
the earth its colors,
a trash can
where a lost cat sleeps.

The skies are gray
like an old man
after a stressful lifetime.

II.

In the day streetlights
sleep
and at night they come on.
They do this because they are nocturnal.

The streets are patiently waiting for someone
to cross them.
The buildings stand
and their legs are tired,
but they can't sit down.
The parks are anxiously waiting
for kids to get out of school.

The cars go back and forth,
not caring where they go
as long as they are fed
with gas.

Johnny Herrera, 13
Everett Middle School

My Mom Was Born in Guatemala

I love my mom. She
is like a best friend for me.
Honest, respectful, friendly, and lovely.
Weekends, we go out together,
to the movies, to eat at nice restaurants,
to the park to take a picture.

Sometimes we fight, but only
for a tiny thing. I still love her.
She is alone. She only
has my little brother and me.

Ana Rodriguez, 14
Everett Middle School

Rain

My hair
softly sifts
through the ocean
while my hands wander over
the city.

As I fall on a hospital,
my eyes at the window
of a delivery room,
I see a young
lady about to give birth.

I reach into the baby.

The baby of rain is now
born and is very healthy
and beautiful.

Yvette Desantiago, 13
Everett Middle School

Angel from Above

My clock is the keeper of time.
My bed is the creator of sleep.
My window is the passage to the unknown.

The TV is my little sister watching
my every move.
The flowers are people's souls.
The VCR is a tax collector.

My pillow is a big, soft hand.
My teddy bear is a baby in a deep rainforest.

I'm an angel from above
sent to lead the way
to peace, joy, and love.

Angelica Ochoa, 14
Everett Middle School

YWCA Mission Girls Services

Snowfall over San Francisco

I descend over car windshields,
over the streets, covering
everything with myself.
I am water where the snow
has melted,
the lightning that breaks
the branch of a tree,
the field of grass
blowing.

Linda Nguyen, 13
Everett Middle School

Rat Boy

Alex tells his parents
he can talk
to rats
and the rats are his
family.

They think he's crazy.

The next morning
he is half-boy
and half-rat.

His parents freak out,
grab their stuff and run.

Mastan Sheik, 13
Everett Middle School

Air

I climb to the top,
thinking I'm getting somewhere,
but all I get are more things
to worry about:
how to please you and the rest
of the world,
slowly losing everything I
ever loved
because you don't think
I deserve it.
Always giving me critical
feedback,
and when I don't want your
feedback, you give more,
stepping on my throat,
taking all of my air.

Jermaine LeBrane, 14
Everett Middle School

Everett Middle School

Everett Middle School

Seeing Myself

I am the boxes of trash
waiting to be taken to the dump.
My emotions
are students laughing,
a book in the old attic.

My eye is a building being painted.

My body is made of flowers
stepped on, shoe marks all over me.
I am the church with singing
bells and trees surrounding me,
a mountain watching planes fly by,
a bird searching for food.

I am a plant seeing my reflection
in a puddle.

Rosy Mena, 13
Everett Middle School

Hunger and Beauty

Hunger
is a lion looking
for a zebra. With short,
messy fur covering its body,
it has crooked nails
and a dirty paw.
Hunger stays
quiet
to wait for its food.

Beauty is a toucan
living on a rainbow
with a sun ray,
trying to see its own reflection.
It wears a beautiful coat
with all the rainbow's colors
and can draw anyone
into a trance.
Beauty is Cupid's helper,
creating
love around the world.

Tung Nguyen, 13
Mercy Services

City Life

I feel myself
awakening finally
in the fragrant cherry blossoms,
in light bouncing from the blood-red
tiles of roofs.

I feel myself dying in the
city horizon,
lead paint peeling,
jet streak,
death bells chiming.

The alphabet of the city
is a water tower,
life
the color of a footstep. My dreams
are crowded
with ivory light and clouds.

City life is a
rose
growing in the crack
of a broken sidewalk.

Elizabeth Thompson, 13
Everett Middle School

Girls After School Academy

My Body

My body is a house
with a rose-tile roof
that protects me from
the piercing rain.

My body
is made of wires
and telephone poles
to allow communication,
to help people cook,
to help businesses work and
supply energy to keep
my body warm.

My body is a bridge
that lets ships go to dock,
to bring goods so that people
survive.

My dreams are trees that express
my feelings.
When I feel good I give out air
to let humans and animals live.

Gruber Tsang, 13
Everett Middle School

Rainy Days at School

As the rain falls like little
mice,
painting a beautiful landscape,
and the street goes black
like sand in Africa,
the J train passes by.

I feel like the wind,
like a jet plane,
swooping with the strength
of a hurricane,
wrestling in a rose and indigo ring,

or gliding like ducks
in a flying **V**.

Chris McMahon, 13
Everett Middle School

My Sad Story

The shattered glass,
the broken windows.
Then a tear.
The spilled juice and food,
the broken dishes.
Then a tear.

The scream, the yell.
Then a tear.
Your fist,
the punch.
Then a tear.
The bruise, cut
and scar.
Then a tear.

Anaia Gilliam, 13
Everett Middle School

This Crazy City

The sirens cry for a chance to reach
the burning building
on its knees for water.
The ringing
of a cell phone tears through your mind,
all the men in their Armani suits
and the women in their bebe skirts.
Cars travel the gray cement
like a school of never-ending fish.

If you take a moment to think,
why is this all here?
Why can't the city just be a closed eye
not seeing anything?

Shahid Minapara, 13
Mercy Services

three Jump

Log Cabin Ranch

The Fourth of July

My heart should be a Roman candle.
Convicts celebrate the Fourth
with T-bone steak
and all the watermelon you can eat.
The irony is bitter
but the melon is sweet,
and though it might be a proud gesture
to refuse the food,
I have more hunger than pride.
So I sit alone
with a slice of melon in my hands,
watching staff
like they watch me.

I ate my heart
to stay alive.
I carved it like meat
and salted it with tears.

I don't care about the calendar.
Whatever day I leave here
will be my Fourth of July.

Like the rest of me
my heart is stubborn.
It tastes like melon on my tongue
and fills my mouth with seeds
and fills my head with seeds
and fills my empty chest with seeds
and I will toil in sorrow,
spitting out my soul like seeds
until my heart grows whole again.

John E. Sweeney, 17
Log Cabin Ranch

Study Harder

In the morning
teacher said

"Study harder
and you'll get a good job"

so from 8 to 5
I studied
and studied
and studied

and when after class
I finally got home
I had much
homework to do

and Mum said
the same thing

"Study harder
and you'll get a good job"

and I said

"Oh! My God!"

Cherry Huang, 16
Newcomer High School

Are You Indian?

They always start out with something nice: "I like your eyes." But then their words come slapping you across the face.

"Are you Indian?" That's what one of them asked me in my wood shop class while I was waiting in line to get my piece of plastic cut. And as soon as I nodded "Yes," he began skipping around in circles, going "OWOOWOOWOOWOOWOOWOO…" "No, not that type of Indian," I said. "I'm the type of Indian that comes from a part of Asia called India."

"Oh, like, how come you don't have, like, a red dot on your forehead?" a girl asked me. "Because I'm Muslim," I said. "The main religion in India is called Hinduism and the girls there wear 'tickas' on their foreheads to represent. I'm not Hindu. I'm Muslim."

"Oh! You're Muslim. Did you have anything to do with those bombings?" another guy asked in a whisper. "Oh, no. You got that from *The Siege*," I said. "That movie literally states that Muslim people are terrorists. Fortunately, you don't see me walking around the city bombing places. And those producers. They should have paid more attention to their seventh-grade social studies class. They would have known what a Muslim is all about. Peace and unity."

Then by the drill machine, some guy asked me, "How come a lot of Indian people be driving cabs?" I was feeling a little annoyed. "Let me guess," I said. "You got that from the Donkey Kong commercial on Nintendo-64, where some disgraceful Indian is standing in front of a busted-up cab saying, 'LOOK WAT HE DEED TO MY CAB!' and begins kicking it, saying, 'AND HE DEEDN'T EVEN TEEP ME!' Not even one person in my family drives a cab and my family isn't big, it's *huge*."

Some girl overheard us and said, "But you can't be Indian because you don't have that accent that Apu does in *The Simpsons*." I was irritated. "You mean, 'Wood yoo like to buy a Slooshee' or 'Oh! Tank yoo, come again'?"

Those are all just stereotypes about those who are like me. Not who I really am.

Sadaf Minapara, 15
Mercy Services

The Ghetto

The ghetto is a place
where nothing's ever mellow
where people say, "What's up?"
instead of saying hello.

Where the poor and the lost grow cold
where guns are shot and drugs are sold
where the cats chase the rats
and the dogs chase them all
from the crack in the sacks
to the macks tryna ball
tennis shoes on the phone pole
spray paint on the wall
laughing children with snotty noses
and stains in their drawers
mothers on welfare
three kids gotta share
two sleep in the bed
the other in the chair.

Underneath there's suffering, hurting, real pain
on the streets it's occurring, minds twirling insane
for the fiends with the addictions
their life is a shame
scream at their children
their wife is to blame
they want it so much
they'll do anything for cocaine
they're on it so much
they forget their own name.

You can run, but can't hide
only some escape
some sold drugs and bought their way out
some showed love and fought their way out
some played hoops and shot their way out
some rapped a demo and hip-hopped their way out
some found family and thought their way out.

But one day, everything will be all settled
one day, maybe one day
everyone will be cool in the ghetto.

Neil B., 17
Log Cabin Ranch

Yellow

I am the light
in your room.
I make your
room beautiful.

I am the sun
that keeps you
warm all the
time.

I am the flower
in your garden
that looks
so beautiful.

I am the taxi.
Ride me every day
and I will bring you
to your destination.

Cherry Mae Brown, 16
Newcomer High School

I Remember

I remember the sight
of the gray of the clouds
in winter and the
waterfall in Guacamayas.

I remember the sound
of my mother's voice
when she screamed to
me in the dark days,
"It is time to go to school."

I remember the taste
of the enchiladas
when the festival
started in the square.

I remember the smell
of the wet soil
when it started to
rain in Michoacán.

I remember the touch
of the hard hands
of my tired father
when he returned
from the farm.

Ignacio Sandoval, 16
Newcomer High School

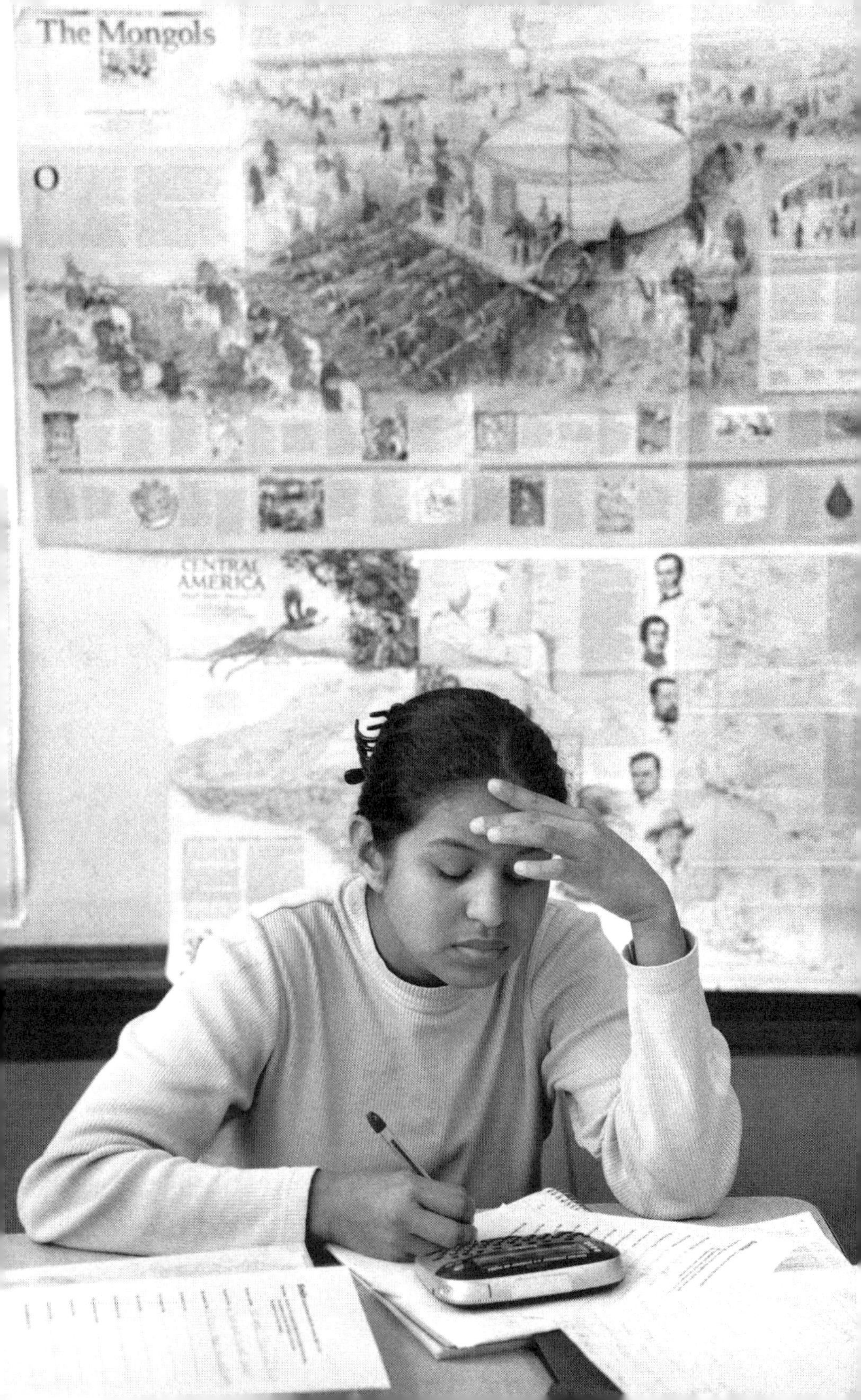

The Mongols
CENTRAL AMERICA

Addiction

I procrastinate and procrastinate.
    I set my life aside
only to be consumed by the manifestations of a maniac
called society.
    Wherever I move, I see agony,
through my own eyes
and in my own heart.
    Paintings on the walls covered with the thoughts
of suffering people.
    My thoughts created my lifestyle,
which shaped the existence of my reality.
    The predicament I put myself in is this prison for the mind.
There is only one way out,
and only one thing to think.
    It's like being subhuman,
a subject of hell.
    Imprisoned by money,
the cause of my own living death.
    Prophets of my future are government statistics,
they add up my life with computers and machines.
    Until the day when my eyes close,
but I'm not asleep.
    Or I get over this disease.

John E. Sweeney, 17
Log Cabin Ranch

Pizza

I loved pizza from the first time I ate it. I don't even remember when I took the first bite.

But at the age of 8, I noticed that my family was eating pizza every day. Mom was working and Dad was like a housewife. When it was dinner time, he would leave his four kids with money to order pizza. I loved pizza, but eating it almost every day was making me sick.

Everything changed in my family after eating pizza more than 30 times a month. One day we found out that Dad was cheating on Mom. Knowing why he always left us with money to order pizza made me sick.

It was three years later when I finally had the stomach to eat pizza again.

Dolly Sithounnolat, 17
Ida B. Wells High School

Bobby

[Standing on a street corner in the Tenderloin, BOBBY sees VAGO's car driving off.]

Damn. He didn't see me. I'm a have to catch him tomorrow.

[BOBBY takes out his wallet. Nothing in it.]

Damn! Hmph. Man, I need some scratch. I can't go looking around like this. Where I'm a sleep tonight? Uh uhhh, I gotta find Vago fast. Even if it takes all night, I gotta get some play. So I can get my hustle on.

[BOBBY puts his wallet back, but notices the picture of his MOM and GIRLFRIEND.]

Damn! Why my moms got to kick me out of the house? I guess she really don't care about me. My girl dumped me, too. Man, my life is real messed up. Right now, I should just kill myself, man! I already know I won't survive on these cold streets, I just know it.

[BOBBY, feeling depressed, crouches down. But then he sees something.]

That car is phat. Look at the chrome wheels on that. That's me, all right. I could just see it now. Me sitting in the driver's seat of a 2000 Mercedes Benz.

[BOBBY puts his arm out as if he's driving.]

With my girl in the passenger seat.

[BOBBY puts his arm around his girl.]

We cruising down the city streets on our way to my mom's house for dinner. And everything's all right!

[BOBBY hears his "Girlfriend" say something.]

"What? Oh, you know it. The usual. Sweet potato pie!"

["She" replies.]

"Yeah! Especially with the whip cream on top and the buttery crust. Uh-uh, mmmm...no one beats my mom's cooking! That's for sure."

[The "car" stops.]

Oh, here we are.
> [BOBBY gets out of car and opens the door for his "Girlfriend." The two walk to the doorway of his "Mom's" apartment building and BOBBY presses the doorbell.]

EEEEE. EEEE.
> ["BOBBY sees his "Mom" coming.]

"We're doing just fine, Momma."
> ["Mom" asks about the car.]

"What? It's my car, Momma."
> ["Mom" asks when he got it.]

"Yeah, Mom. I bought it last week."
> ["Mom" asks where the money is from.]

"Well, you know, I've been working downtown at the uh, uh...big-time offices."
> ["Mom" asks when.]

"I just started a couple of weeks ago."
> ["Mom" suspects he's lying.]

"Mom, Mom, I'm not lying. I'm not."
> ["Mom" accuses him of dealing.]

"I'm not dealing with Vago, Momma! I stopped that..."
> ["Mom" is going to call the police.]

"Don't call the police, please don't."
> ["Mom" shuts the door in his face. BOBBY wakes up to the fact that he's still on the streets.]

Damn...I know she loves me, though. I'll just have to wait for the right time to start begging her if I could come back home. But for now, I'm tryin' to ball till I fall. I'm gonna be higher than Vago. He's gonna be coming to me pretty soon.
> [Beat.]

But I have to start fresh first.
> [BOBBY runs off.]

Neil B., 17
Log Cabin Ranch

My Feelings

I am a sad princess.
I wonder why we are here.
I hear the sound of the rain.
I see a world full of wickedness.
I want to be a person certain of myself.
I am a sad princess.

I pretend to be a strong person.
I feel bad when I don't understand some things.
I touch my face and I see I'm valuable.
I worry about how I will feel at my end.
I cry for my father; he needs me.
I am a sad princess.

I understand everything has a price in the world.
I say, "I know I can do this!"
I dream one day I will go back to my country.
I try to calm my attitude.
I hope one day I will see my old friends.
I am a sad princess.

Evelyn Morales, 17
Newcomer High School

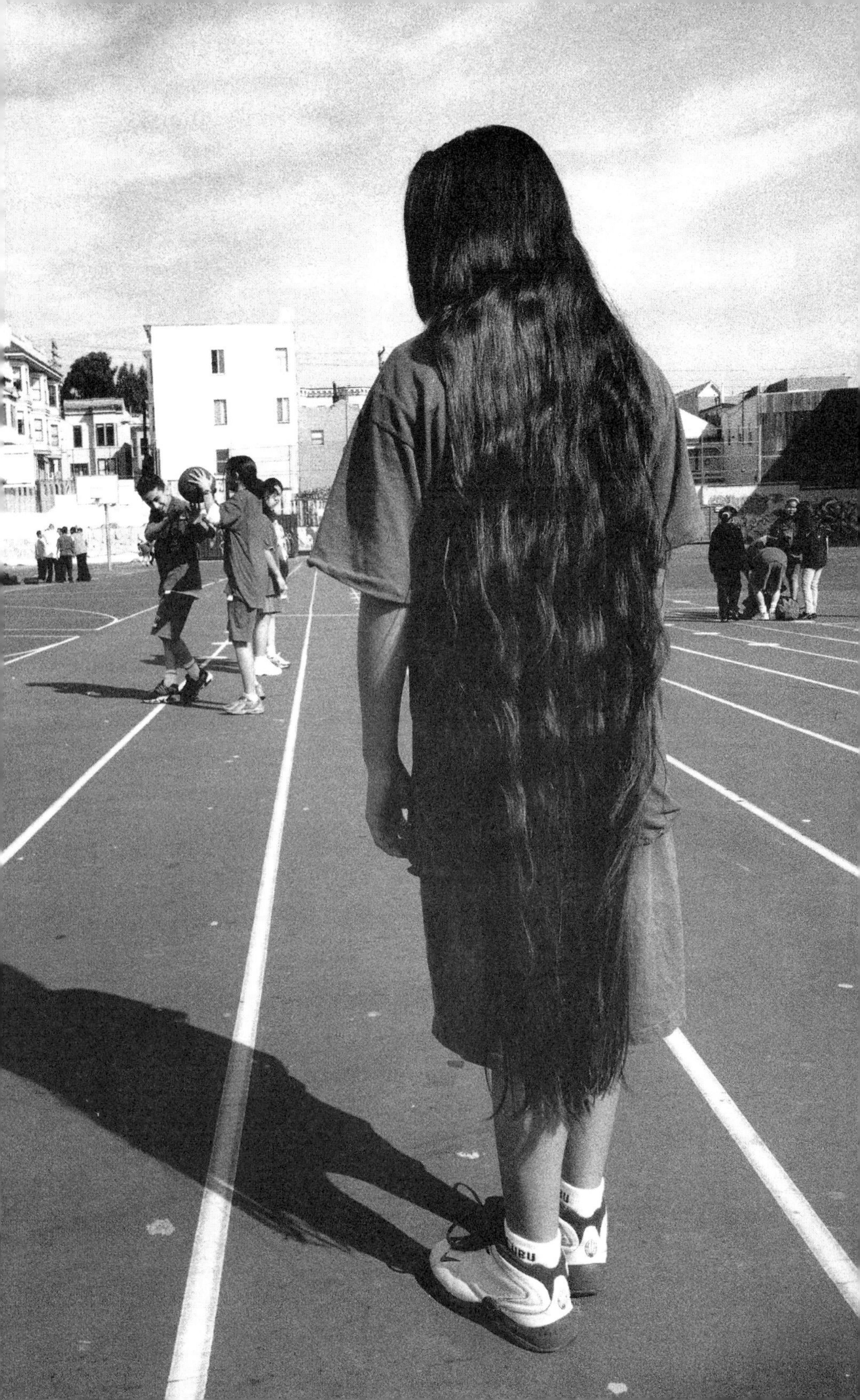

How to Be a Little Sister

You always are a "little one"
like a dolly for your folks.
You always have to be dear
and keep your face innocent,
even when something happens
and it's your fault.
Try to do the things
that your sister has to do,
so she will allow you
to go out with friends.
Don't open your mouth
even when you know
something incredible about her,
so she won't tell anybody
that you took Mom's make-up for a party.
Be nice to your sister
and make her fruit salad
when you want to
borrow her cool shirt
for a date with your new boyfriend.

Sometimes I think that
I'm lucky I don't
have a little sister.

> Inna Stukova, 17
> Newcomer High School

Shy

You look like the setting sun, so beautiful.
You also look like a bride, so delicately pretty.
Generous is your bridegroom. He can protect you.
Do you know we like to see you when you look like a red peach?
Do you know when you look like the setting sun,
the world becomes a romantic picture?
You make many people want to protect you.

Chia Ling Peng, 16
Newcomer High School

Tai Shang

I always like fall best.
You can eat moon cakes
with your family in the open air
and admire the moon together
on Mid-Autumn Day.
At harvest time,
you are streaming with sweat.
At last, you feel tired.
Then, you lie under a tree,
nice and cool breeze.
You watch the sky,
the splendid and blue sky.
Little by little,
you get into your own dream.

Da Cheng Li, 16
Newcomer High School

Newcomer High School

Mental Torment

Sitting still in the corner,
a knock at the door.
Sitting still in the corner,
a rapping at my door.

A creature enters.
"Did you not hear me
rapping at your door?"
Silent laugh,
black stained glass,
tinted mirrors,
all in pretty, messy rows.

The bird chirps, the little girl cries,
the mirrors break, the little girl falls.
She bleeds, the floor runs red with rage,
pretty shiny, crystal clear. Red runs
wild, I lean over and paint myself red.

For an instant, I feel peace at last.
Red, red rage runs down my face.
I stand, look into the mirrors and
see a shattered little girl.

                Jackie Cabrera, 16
              Ida B. Wells High School

Urban Life

The strangest phrase of amazement
is the revolution to befriending.

Seeking to recognize the importance
of respect for light in the mirror,
you're one of his soul love body forms.

Moon sets,
water falls,
a good location for ignorance to be pulled down
and be gone.

This twisted mind state is a death
from no responsibility.
To explode is a poison waste,
you encounter the prison rate.

Crushing the national habitat is leaving
prison footprints.
This melting thought-
obliterating, a thousand souls
and the re-creation of light
is gone.

Andrew E., 17
Log Cabin Ranch

Ode to My Sister Zulma

Zulma is the best sister
in the whole world.
She never leaves me alone.
She just wants the best for me.
She doesn't imagine how much I love her.
She works so hard,
She's so loving.
When she gets home tired from working,
she's still nice, kind, and especially lovely.
She treats me as if she were my mother.
She trusts me so much.
She knows how to keep a secret.
She's always there when I need her.
She never regrets things that she does.
She's so clever,
she knows what she wants.
The only thing I want
is to tell her that I love her
and I would like to be beside her forever.

Karen Valenzuela, 16
Mission High School

My Father

Now that I'm gone, how do you feel?
Does it make you upset that our relationship
changed because I'm gone? Now you feel grief
and loss because I'm gone. You have all
the time to think about the things you done in the past
and you wish it never happened.
Did you really think your ways of evil
and alcoholism solved problems? Or was it
the way you listened to Carlos Santana
in a muscle shirt and shorts, chain-smoking
Camels, beating on the table as you were
one with the music. Did you think you
were the King? What kind of King are you
now that there's no prince to command?
Multiple personalities all through my life.
I'm surprised you don't have love and hate tattooed
on your broad hairy knuckles. Was it your job
that gave you gray hairs, that were once black as
coal when you guzzled the tall can?
It always started from two cents
and I watched it escalate to 100 bucks of nothing
but alcohol-enraged actions. I hated when
you talked to me by spitting
on my face and I smelled your alcohol-infested breath.
What happened to you as a child? Am I
going to inherit it from you? Am I going to
act like you, so-called King of the House?
I don't think you like reality,
the truth hurts.

Craig F., 16
Log Cabin Ranch

Newcomer High School

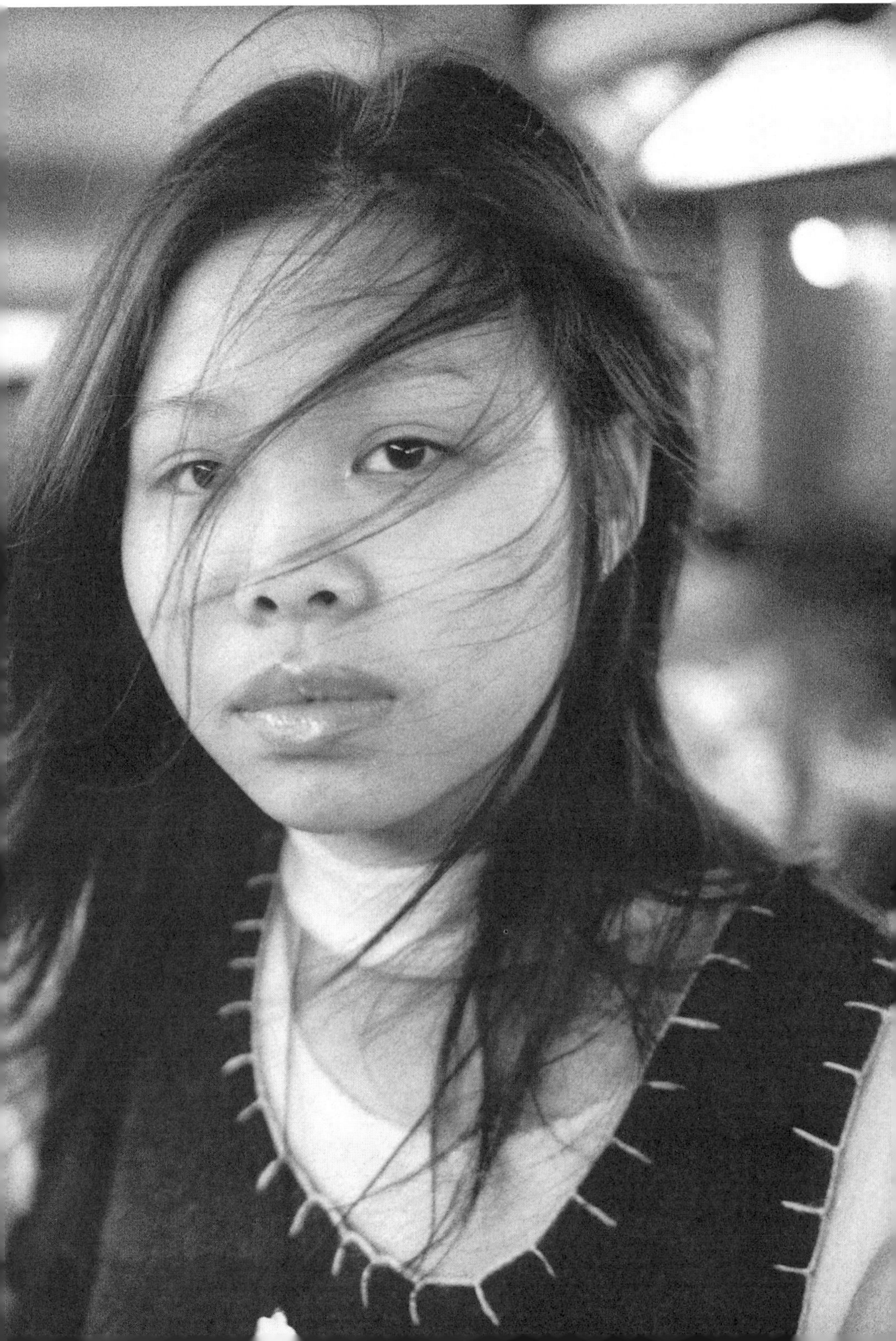

Poetry

Poetry is the soft whispers
of the women gossiping in the living room.

She is the flowerpot
on the kitchen windowsill.

She is the sound of the radio
telling the daily news

and the forbidden tunes flying in the air.

She is the spices
being dropped in the boiling curry
sending a shocking smell to the hungry
men on the balcony.

Poetry is the girl
hidden underneath the bed
eating sweets from the plastic teacup.

She is the sneaky cat jumping
from roof to roof knocking
the clothes down from the clothesline.

>Asefa Subedar, 15
>Mercy Services

Newcomer High School

Questions for the Great Wall

How many years have you stood there?

Are you still a child or an old man?

How do you feel when you see the world?

Happy or lonely?

Who uncovered your mysterious veil?

How many kinds of colors do you have on your body?

Just one, or more colors?

Do you mind if a person calls you "Chinese Mother"?

Cathy She, 17
Newcomer High School

The Right Side of Upside Down

I start up when my eyes open,
but my attention span is down
'cause I don't know nothing.
I rise up
'cause I grow up.
I learn piece by piece.
Life. Love. Care.
When will I stop getting cold feet?
My life rises from grade to middle to high to the universe.
Through my life I know all discipline through hurt.
Is my future burnt?
Is this life a curse?
Could the system tell I was a criminal at birth?
Have they been looking at me since my first breath?
Would I leave this Earth of Being, incarcerated to death?
I grew from an eight-pound clown.
When I touch down,
will the right side still be upside down?

DeAngelo R., 17
Log Cabin Ranch

Pomegranate   Just like flower smell from far away,
it must taste good,
this fire-red-skin fruit.

It looks like a flower getting ready to bloom.
Maybe it's one eye of fire dragon.
Ah, or a meteor dropping from the dark sky.

Song Zhao Gong, 15
Newcomer High School

Tulips

I remember
when I was living in Florida, my grandmother had a whole big thing of flowers.
They were tulips and they were in front of the house.
We all would wake up in the morning to the smell of flowers.
It would just rush over our noses to wake us up to the fresh air,
and I'd just feel good all day, all ready to go to school feeling like 1 million dollars.
It would make me feel good all day and night, day after day, the same smell.
You just could not get tired of that smell.
It smelled like I imagine heaven would smell like.

Ricky Hernandez, 17
Ida B. Wells High School

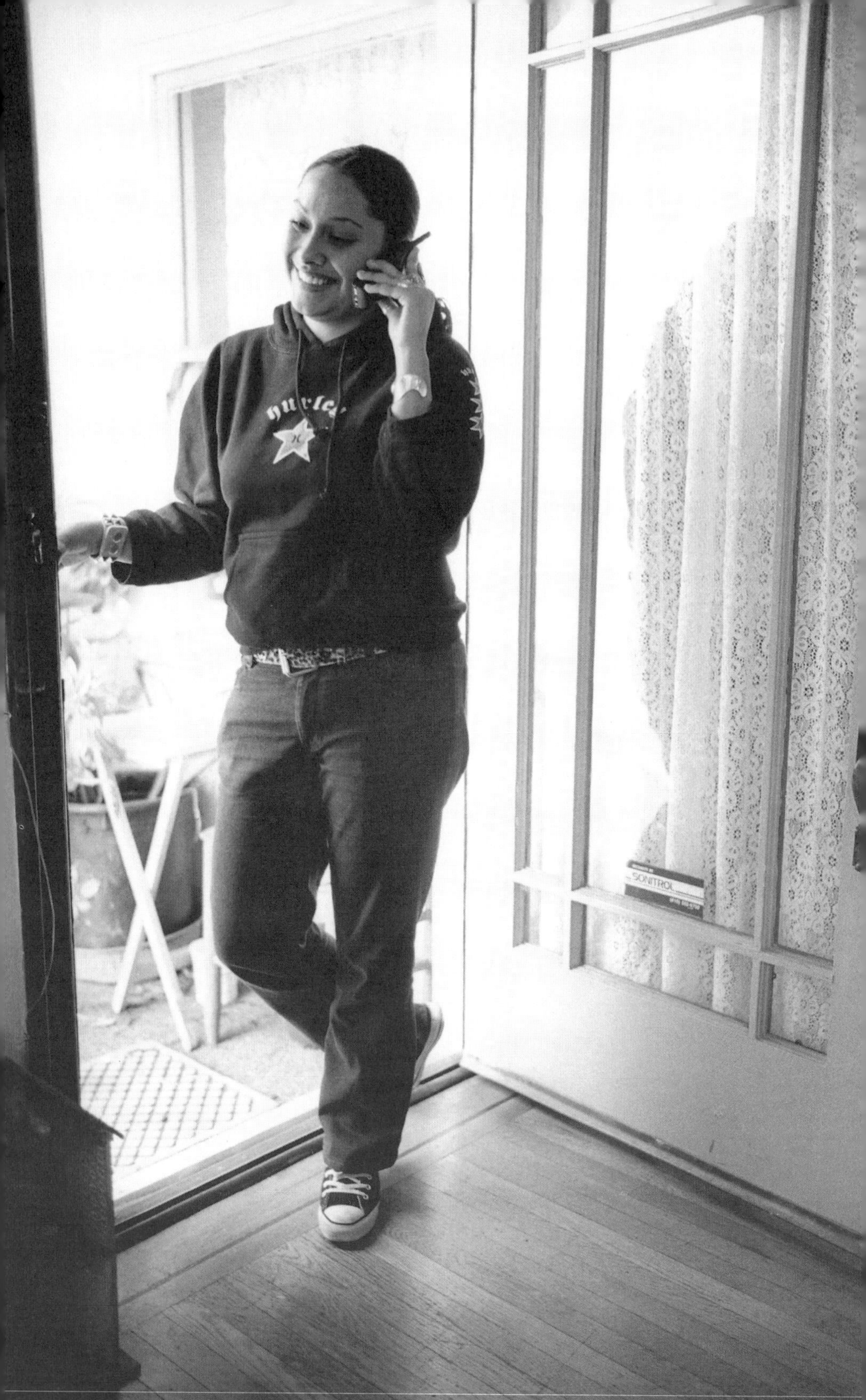
SONITROL

Me

I am a happy and lovable girl.
I wonder about the final exam.
I hear the star sound of the sky.
I see porpoises at the sea's bed.
I want to fly in the sky.
I am a lovable and happy girl.

I pretend to be a naughty girl.
I feel a hundred flowers bloom in the summer.
I touch the beautiful moon.
I worry my dog will die.
I cry for my grandmother.
I am a lovable and happy girl.

I understand how to draw the pictures.
I say, "We will be friends."
I dream I will go to space.
I try to make the paper crane.
I hope everything is okay.
I am a lovable and happy girl.

LiLi Liang, 16
Newcomer High School

My Chrysanthemum Tea

I can smell the tea.
Its taste is very good.
It is sour, but it is a little sweet also.
So I want to smell it again and again.
There is something that appears in my memory.
I remember my mother made chrysanthemum tea for us.
In summer, my mother liked to make it after lunch.
When you drank it, you would feel very cool.
I no longer drink it; my family has moved to America.
But the taste still stays in my memory.

Kristy Ruan, 16
Newcomer High School

Grandmom

Grandmom was the taste of candy.
She was happy as a clown.
She was like looking at a sunrise in the morning.
She dressed me every morning like her doll.
My grandmom is with me like a shadow.

Christy Allen, 17
Ida B. Wells High School

Poetry

Poetry should be the last rosy clouds in the sunset,
streak her red lipstick across the sky
when you feel sad.

Poetry should be a benevolent grandma,
gently touch my heart
when my mother blames me.

Roger Duan, 16
Newcomer High School

Newcomer High School

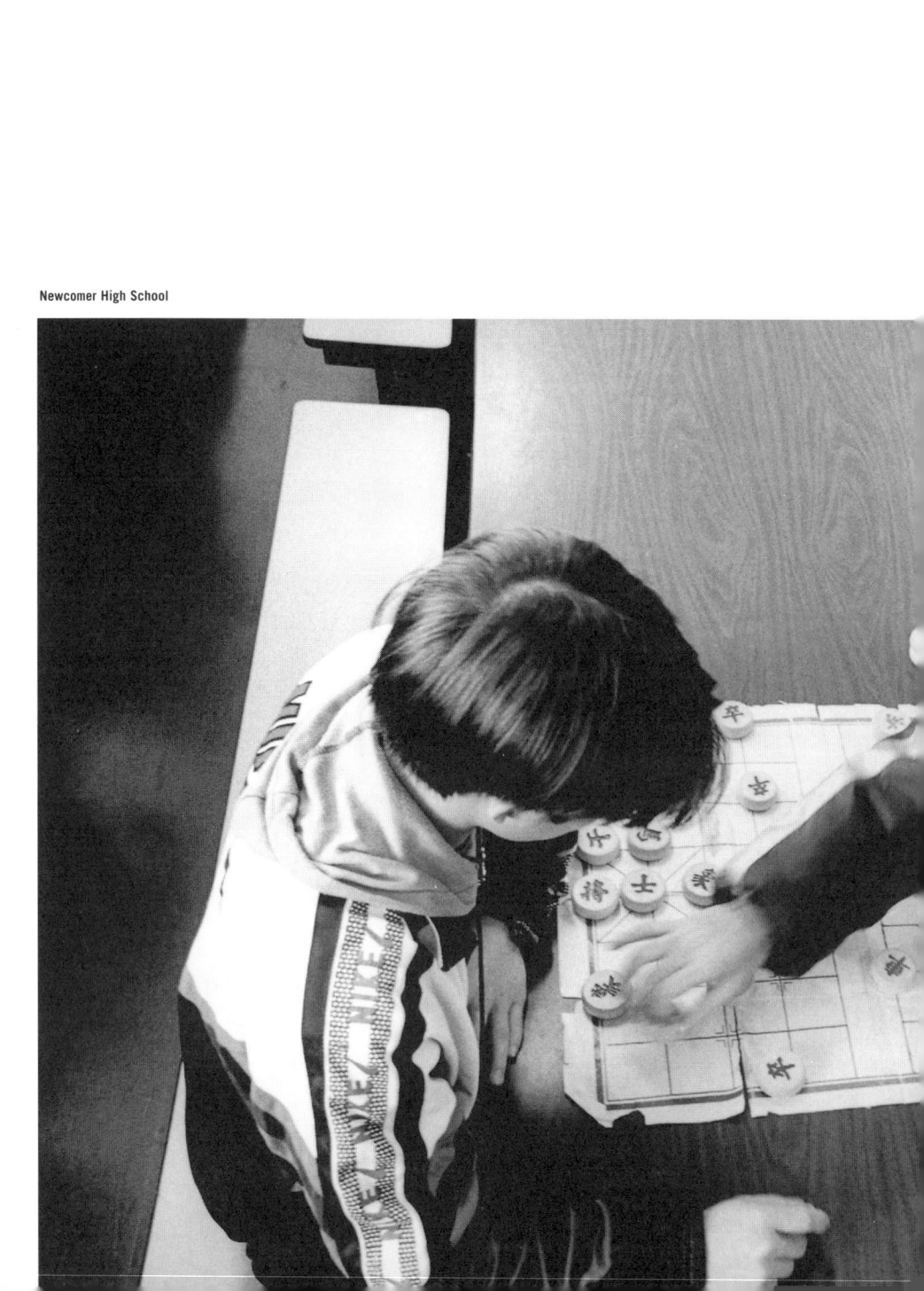

Okra

I hate okra.
I would never eat it.
It makes me sick.
My grandmother often puts it in gumbo,
but I hate it.
I would never eat okra,
not even for money.
It tastes that bad.
If I had to choose between eating okra
and wearing a turtleneck,
I'd choose the turtleneck.

Angelo Richardson, 16
Ida B. Wells High School

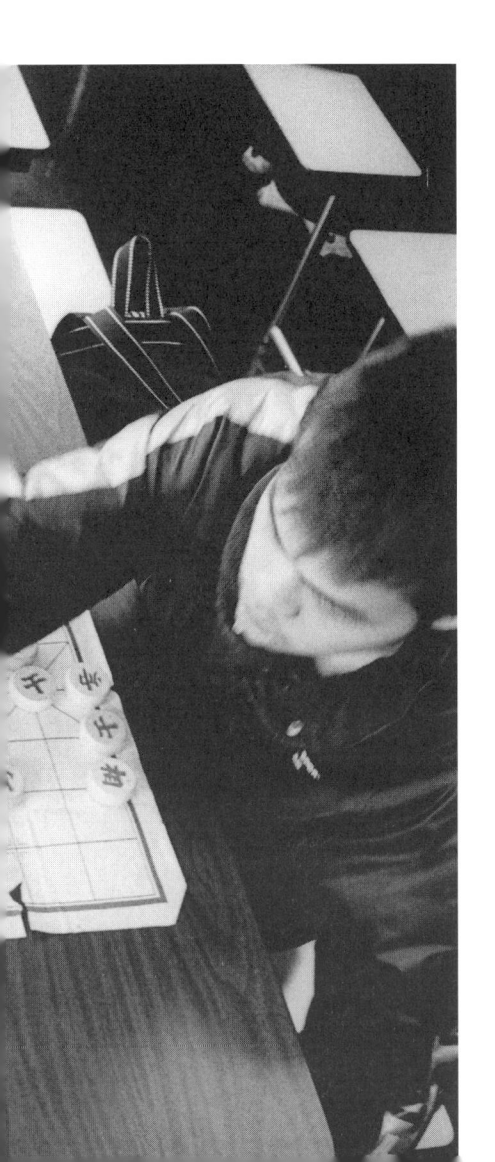

Grandma

I remember the sight,
an old and small flat.
She always worked in
the kitchen.

I remember the sound.
She always called my
name when I was
so noisy.

I remember the taste
when we had
dinner together. And I liked
the hometown chicken very much.

I remember the touch
when she grasped my head
when I left Hong Kong.
"Take care," she said.
And my grandma was going to cry for me.

Janie Fung, 16
Newcomer High School

The Crush

When I think someone is cute,
I look not only at their outside appearance,
but their inside.
I remember once,
when I was in fourth grade,
I was partnered up with
the biggest nerd in school.
After about two days
of sitting next to him,
I started to notice his eyes.
And when he would correct me
on my work,
I thought that was cute.
So I had a crush on him
for about a week,
but I knew he was never into me.

Vanessa Soriano, 18
Loco Bloco

In My Past Life

In my past life,
I was a frog in the well.
I didn't know how the world is.
It's big, small, or huge?
I just stayed in the well.
In my past life,
I was the seed under the soil.
I was afraid if I go out,
I would feel cold.
I just hid under the soil.
I didn't have any friends to talk to me.
I felt alone.
In my past life,
I was a plantlet.
I was growing in a small park.
I wasn't beautiful.
Everybody liked the beautiful flowers.
They enjoyed them, not me.
But I didn't give up.
I believed that I would grow more beautiful than the others.
In my past life,
I was the water.
I wanted to flow into the sea
and help the farmers irrigate their plants.

Cindy Wu, 16
Newcomer High School

four **Leap**

What Poetry Should Be

Poetry should be a scripture
       an essay, writing words,
         a feeling: love, hate, anger.
Whatever you want to call it,
poetry should be about whatever you
put down on a piece of paper,
as long as you have 500 words in your head
in a day.
Poetry should be about what you go through in a day—
what your life is about,
what you experience,
what you see,
things that are real
and imagined.
It's more than words on a paper,
it comes from inside.

            Anwar Collins, 18
            Ida B. Wells High School

Log Cabin Ranch

Are You Doing That New Drug Thing?

Inspired by Juan Felipe Herrera's "Are you doing that new Amerikan thing?"

>Are you doing that new drug thing?
>Walkin' around not knowing where you're going thing?
>Wasting all your money on that
>magical green plant thing.
>Are you doing that puff-puff-pass thing?
>Little boys and little girls trying to be grown thing.
>It's a do it at lunch every day thing.
>Is it an addiction thing?
>It's really a stupid thing.
>
>>Michael Currie, 18
>>Ida B. Wells High School

Take It Back
Inspired by Sekou Sundiata's "Shout Out"

Here is to all the people who are negative,
racist people who try to hold everyone back
from completing their God-given mission.
You will soon be stopped and erased.
Because as time goes on people learn from their mistakes,
and soon all races will take back their freedom.

Here is to the U.S. government,
which has put us into a mental jail cell.
This will all blow up in your face
as the people will take the government back.

Angelo Phillips, 18
Ida B. Wells High School

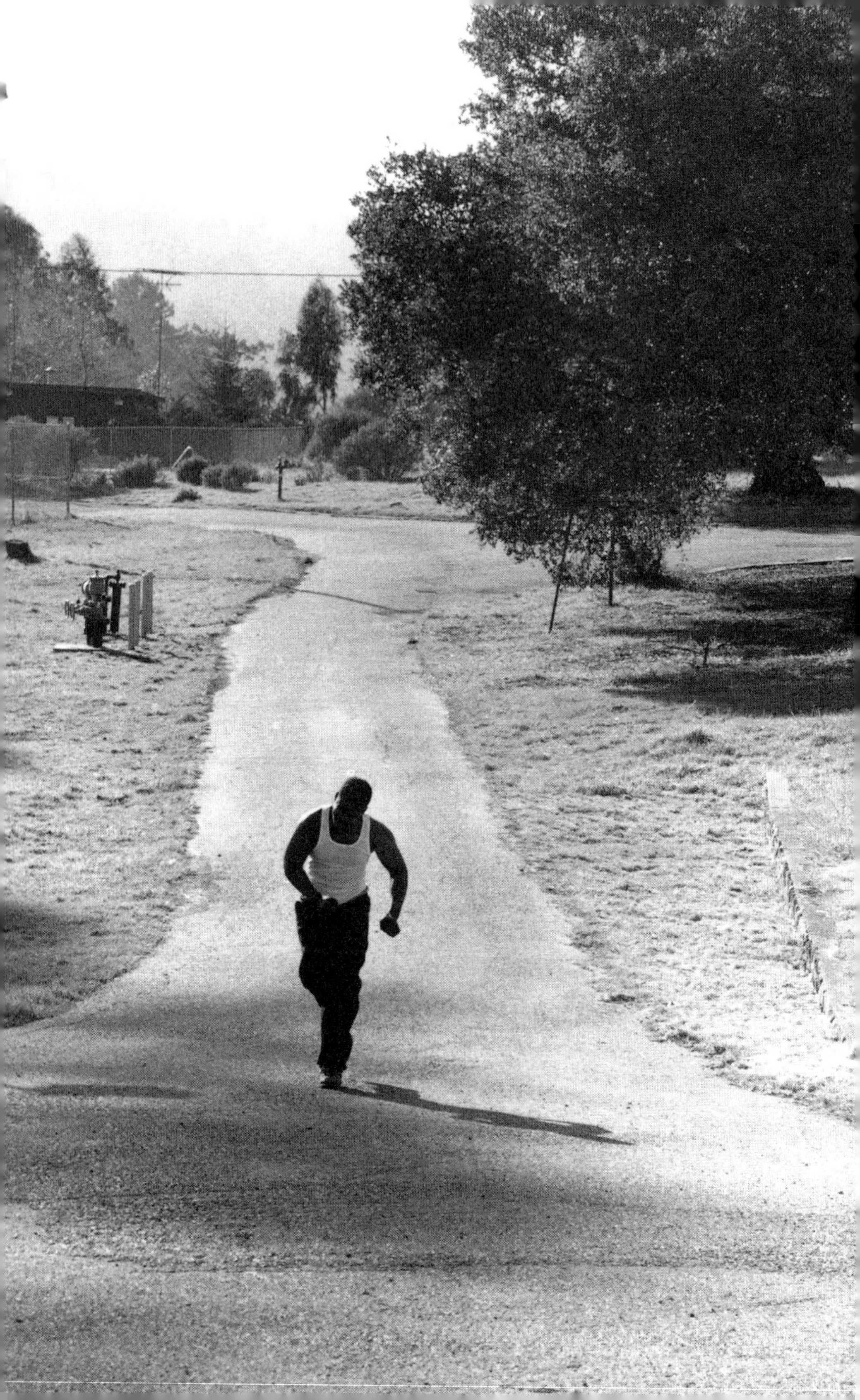

Regret

Keep doing what
I do, I find
myself in a ditch.
Electric chairs,
ropes around my body,
clinched.

I want to live
life full of respect.
Things I done did
I will always
regret.

Everick S., 18
Log Cabin Ranch

Ain't Nobody Understands Me

People say they understand, but they really don't,
so I go on with my life and leave what they said behind.
They tell me they got love fa me, but
lie to me 'cause they really despise me.
I goes to court to get sentenced by the judge
who says the place I'm being sent to is good,
to help change my lifestyle. He smiles at me,
but under that mask he put on
is a face of putting lives to death.
But no one understands me.
My days are not able to be seen 'cause
of the darkness that's blockin' the light
to shine in and set me free
so other people would understand me.
But fa people to understand me is very complicated,
like a Rubix cube and blowing air
into an air balloon using yo lungs to make it huge.
Ain't no one understands me.

Daniel A., 18
Log Cabin Ranch

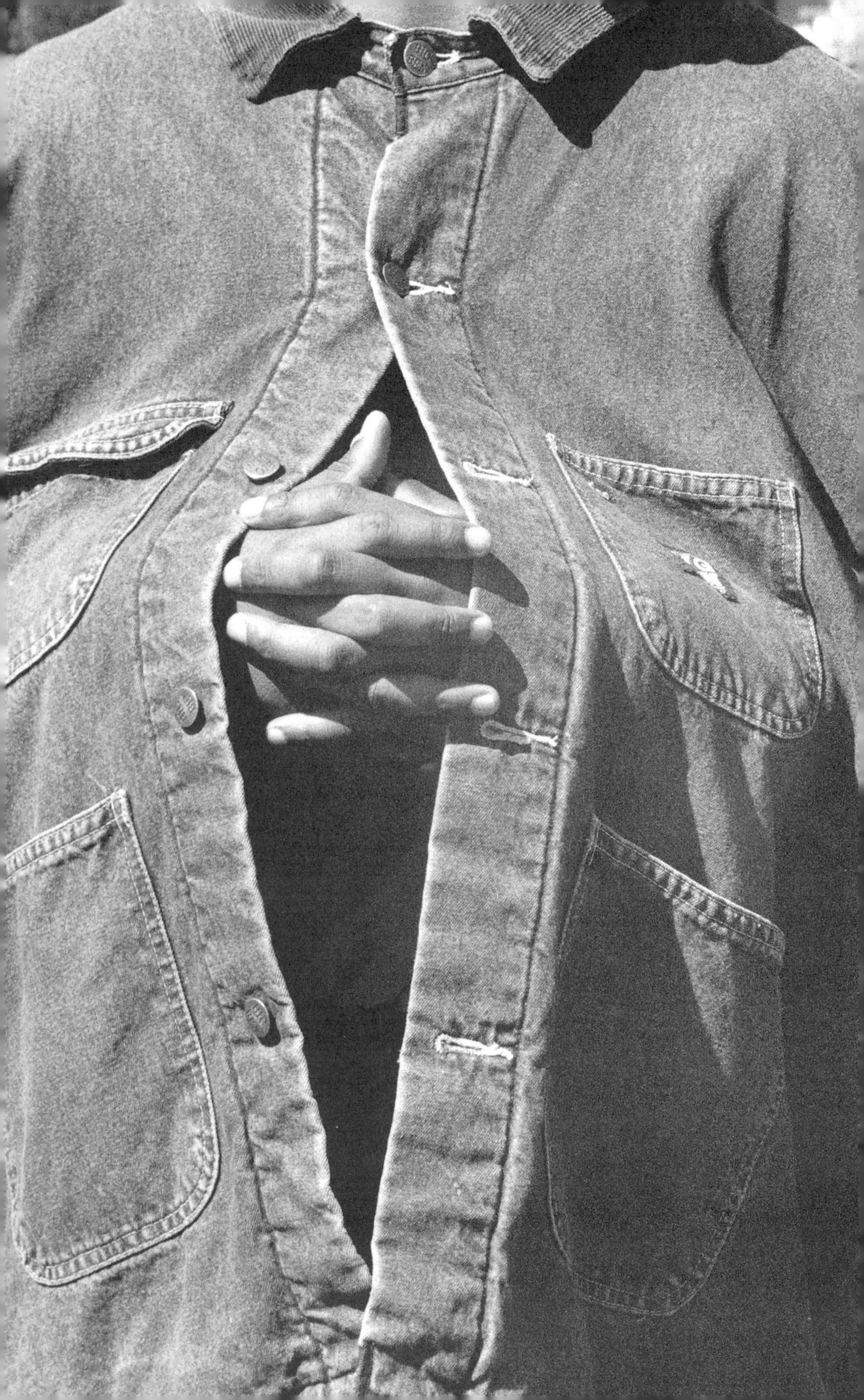

YWCA Mission Girls Services

Indian Spirit

As I lie in my bed
I listen to the spirits
that wander at night.
Suddenly I hear my grandma's voice
calling for me.
I open my eyes
seeking her like an owl
stalking his prey.
But I don't see her.
My eyes get watery
and tears start flowing like rivers.
I picture her in my head,
her black hair,
her brown skin,
representing the great Indian
that she was.

                          Octavio S., 19
                          Log Cabin Ranch

Haiku Leaves taste the springtime
falling from the tops of trees.
Everything I dream   becomes.

Ignacio Sanchez, 18
Ida B. Wells High School

Haiku Spring comes,
very soft and warm
like my mother.

Karen Au, 18
Newcomer High School

Abandoned

This life I live
been messed up since I was a kid.
Hated my father cuz of the dirty thangs he did.
He left my mom cuz she said she is goin' to have me.
As soon as he heard that, he got on
cuz he didn't want to take the responsibility.

I met him once or twice
and he seemed to be nice.
I couldn't figure him out
cuz he was unpredictable,
like the roll of a pair of gamblin' dice.

I don't know why he left,
but now I don't care
cuz he wasn't there
since I first took my breath.
He didn't take his child in his arms to rest
and hold him close to his chest,
makin' an undyin' commitment
to love him till death.

I don't know why this guy
made my mom cry and hurt inside,
and told her she was havin' nothin' but a lie,
that it was just an accident that night
and it's not worthy to be alive.

I do not know the whole story,
but I give the man upstairs the glory
that he gave my mom the strength to born me.

He ain't my father.
As I got older
I don't bother thinkin' about that sucka
cuz my real father is the one who married my mother
and gave me sisters and brothers
and gives me hope when I'm sinkin' in the gutter.

He's my stepfather.
I love him to death
for bein' with me every step of the way,
and my mother Maggievay
who brightens
my day.

                                Daniel A.
                                Log Cabin Ranch

A Poem for the Man

I wanna rob you of your riches
and take back the land you stole.
Stop the poor from being poor,
but we all know
that ain't happening anymore.

I wanna walk up to Capitol Hill,
scream out your name
and let the people know
that you ain't got no game.

I wanna organize against you,
get all my folks together
and come at your ass
like some icy weather.

Turn your prisons into schools,
your corporations into homes,
so that all my people will be finally free to go.

I wanna educate the people
and let it be known
that we have an evil man on the prowl—
you heard, we have an evil man on the prowl.

He looks like Proposition 21,
dressed to impress you in reports of youth crime.
He sounds like Proposition 227,
talking no more BI-lingual education,
it's about time.

He steps on toes
with his big cowboy boots called welfare reform
and calls out, "If you wanna live, you need to conform."

I wanna make my own most-wanted list
for crimes against the people,
and when we catch him,
we ain't making any deals.

Marlene Sanchez, 20
Center for Young Women's Development

Hell of Angels

The Angel tells me
to listen and I will be safe.
My bones ache, but praying
will be necessary,
and I say already there are too many
echoes in me,
and I say I have been in shadow too long!
So there weeping in the corner
can cause harsh emotion
and sadden feelings,
but still helplessly needing help
and support
in my shadow.

        Robert C., 19
        Log Cabin Ranch

One and Only

She is the one
who gets you up
at the waking of dawn.

She is the one
who shields you
from the harsh winds on a rainy day.

She bundles
you tight, pointing you on the right path.

She is a blanket,
there to share her warmth.

She is the unsuspecting pair of eyes
that watches your every move.

She is, she is
a mother.

    Anastasia
    Ida B. Wells High School

Girls After School Academy

Our Year

This is the year that we rise to the occasion.
Our will is strong,
we gonna free this nation.

This year we're changing the rules, so you better watch out.
Through our struggles rose power,
we gonna do more than shout.

This year we stop prison guards in their tracks.
Grab the keys.
Unlock the shackles.
Take our loved ones back.

This is the year we're not settlin' for scraps.
We're takin' what's ours,
no questions asked.

This is the year they prayed would never come.
In defense they planted poison seeds of picket fences
and unattainable American dreams,
not once thinking that their master plan was weak at the seams.

But it was, and this year we're bustin' it open,
takin' back the land that they know is stolen.

This is the year our people will rise,
free our brothers and sisters without fear in our eyes.

Jessica Nowlan-Green, 21
Center for Young Women's Development

Praise the Blue-Collared

Here's to the hard working-class people,
set up in this twisted system.
Working hard to pay bills and survive
while the government takes out what they call
"taxes."

Here's to the hard working-class people,
who make people they shall never know
far richer than any working-class men can be.

Here's to the hard working-class people,
who deal with everyday problems
like catching the bus and getting home safely
while the rich people drive their Benzes and Land Rovers
and park in their three-car garages.

Here's to the hard working-class people,
whose hands are brittle from work
while rich people get manicures
on their soft uncalloused palms.

Here's to the hard working-class people,
who continue to persevere
despite all the challenges.

Here's to the hard working-class people.

Raoul Tom, 18
Ida B. Wells High School

1/20/90 -- 06/05/00

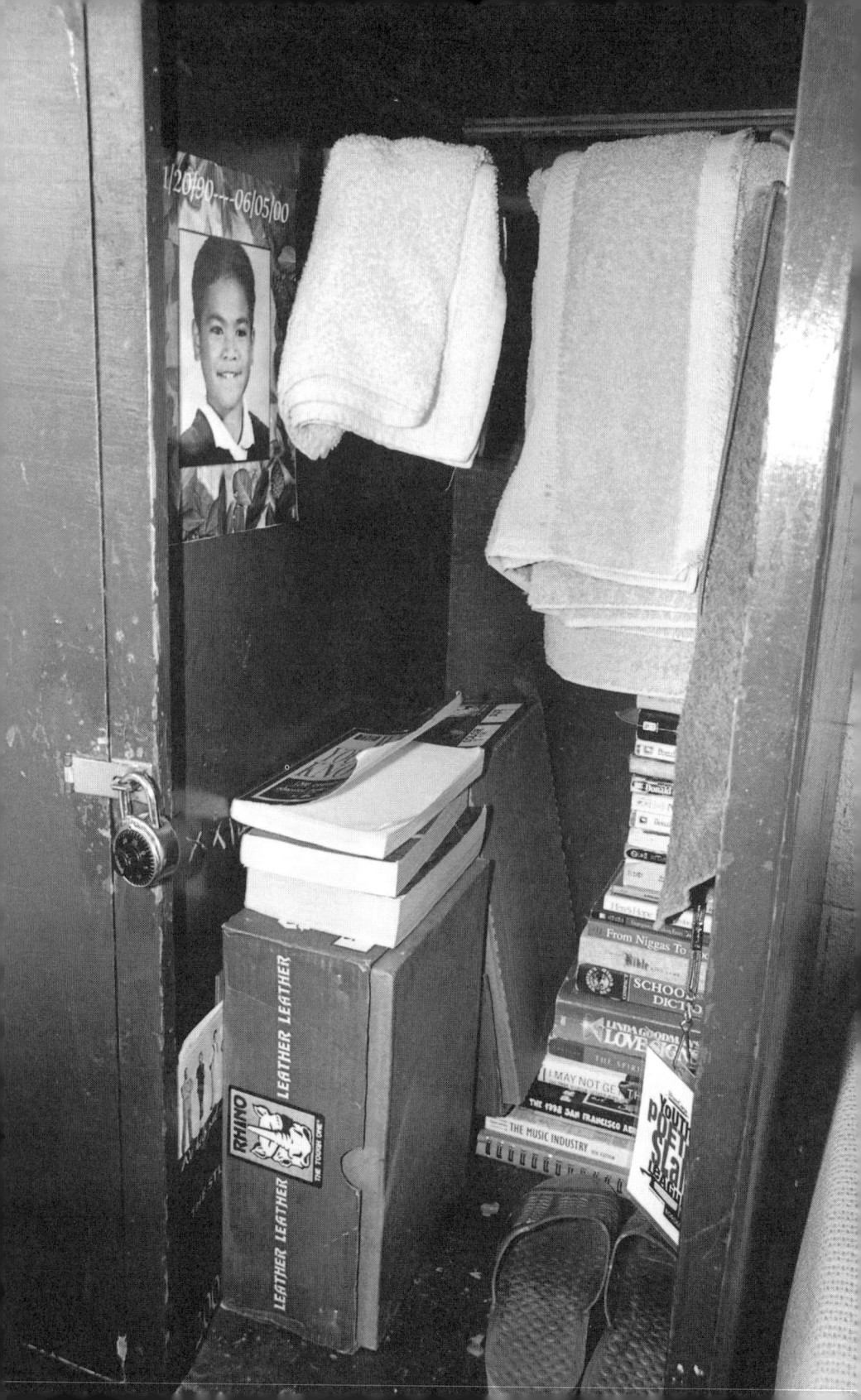

Love Poem for Home

Home tastes like cold milk with ice cubes
and Italian dressing that dripped from the salad
to the pasta,
that got stuck in the rigatoni
and is tangy on my tongue.
Home tastes like red cherry Kool-Aid
with not enough sugar
out of an old mayo jar.
Tastes like mayonnaise and white bread,
and orange juice on my cereal
when I had no milk.

Love sounds like my husband's voice
calling my name
just to make sure I'm still there.
Sounds like my nails
against his stubbly scratchy cheeks.

My love
sounds like my baby's voice
trying to talk to me
and tell me his thoughts,
sounds like the clanging of forks on plates
after a good meal,
and my daughter
sweet singing when her headphones are on
and she thinks no one is listening.

Jessica Nowlan-Green, 21
Center for Young Women's Development

Family Night Out

The moon is out
and the kids makin' funny noises with their mouth.
Aunts, uncles, nephews, nieces, mom and dad, brothers, sisters
are at Grampa's farm in a circle
in the cold keeping each other warm.
The animals in the woods, howling and growling,
while me and the folks smiling and clowning.
I'm on the tree looking in the sky
and see the twinkling stars,
glad to be out from them stanky ol' bars.
The trees are swaying and the kids are playing,
Grandma in the house cookin' and bakin'.
It's a beautiful night and the family is tight.
We all goin' to stay up all night until the moon goes down
and the sun comes up
and shines his light.

>Daniel A., 18
>Log Cabin Ranch

five **Soar**

teachers' writings

When I Forget Why I Teach

I think of the time we were writing about grandmothers,
how they never seemed to believe in purses,
instead tucked what is precious behind bra straps.

One girl told us about her nani
in the village near Bombay,
the stash of rupees she buried deep in her bosom.

I remembered my bubbe, the handkerchief
she pulled out Friday nights when it graced her head
like the blessing she would say over the candles.

And you, Inez, girl who swears she cannot write poems.
Somewhere in that black-and-white composition notebook
between the scrawled litany of boys' names

and the algebra homework you never turned in,
you found your abuelita in her rose garden in Jalisco,
and the small tin heart she pinned against her own.

What do they call those in English? you asked me. I forget.
Milagro, my Spanish dictionary said.
Miracle.

                    Alison Seevak
                    Newcomer High School
                    Mercy Services

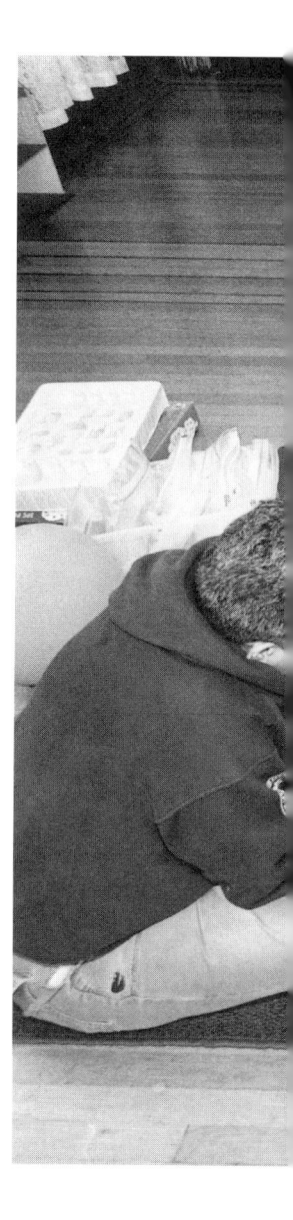

YWCA Mission Girls Services

Breaking Ground

*Roses are red,
Violets are blue,
Sugar is sweet
and so are you.*

I've been talking to third to fifth graders about poetry while they're eating lunch, cutting and pasting, cooling off in the halls. It seems that every time I introduce myself as a poet, someone begins to recite: "Roses are red, violets are blue…" By the tenth time I find myself thinking, *If I hear that one more time, I'm going to bop you!*

But in a way I'm thankful. Knowing a poem by heart, one they can whip out of their jeans pockets and offer easy as candy, neatly wrapped and sticky-sweet, gives these children a handle on poetry, a sense of ownership.

Still, is this really a good starting point for launching a creative writing program? I imagine students giving voice to their fears of walking home in unsafe neighborhoods, their longing for absent fathers and mothers, their fragile wishes and dreams. *Roses are red, violets are blue?* Poems like this, I think, give poetry a bad name. Poems like this teach kids to plaster over their true voices with cute, rhyming wallpaper. How could I peel back the sticky layer of roses and sugar, of what children think they are supposed to or allowed to say, to get to the secret words growing inside like bones?

At recess today I sit on a log bordering the new garden, a garden formed by smashing through the concrete playground surrounding the school. Outside the high fence, family houses rub shoulders. On one side of Mission Street a market with a sign in Chinese sells durians, on the other a store with a sign in Spanish offers fat Mexican papayas. Inside the fence, flowers, like children, dot the gray landscape of fog and pavement with color. Listening to shouts of "You're it!" and "My turn!", I wonder how to carve out a home for poetry here. Where will I find space in a school where supplies and rooms are scarce and dedicated teachers are already pushed to the limit? Will there be room for wild, overgrown voices—*roses are squishy, violets are sleep*—in the margins of essays and times tables?

Three Latina girls approach, all smiles and need. "Who are you?" asks Teresa, balancing on the log gymnast-style. When I explain I am a poet, her face lights up. "I know a poem!" she announces, stretching up tall. "Roses are red, violets are blue…" The other two start to join in, but Teresa pauses, trying to remember a funny version her brother told her. And in that moment I feel the concrete walls begin to crack, a sprout of hope peeking through. In that moment of forgetting, the poem can go anywhere. There is freedom to say anything, even something you didn't mean to say, didn't know you were capable of saying.

To Teresa, her face scrunched up with effort, it's a hard place to be. "Let's make something up," I suggest. The other girls try to help by rattling off the variations they've heard—"Roses are red, violets are blue, sugar is sweet and so is maple syrup." Not bad. "Violets are blue, roses are red, you wet your bed and fell on your head." Hmmm. Not exactly Langston Hughes. "How about a different kind of love poem," I say. "A love poem to…?"

"Your tongue!" a voice shouts, preceding an overalled girl with a thick black braid, her tongue already sticking out. Two Asian American girls inch closer. A boy stops bouncing a ball to listen. A love poem to your tongue? It's irresistible. "O tongue," I begin, and someone immediately adds, "you are so slimy and long." Giggles. "Like what?" I ask. "Like slimy goo…like a slide…like a snake swimming in ice cream…" and the hard walls surrounding the garden of poetry begin to crumble.

Tomorrow my new students will go out to the playground on a treasure hunt, bringing back words for what they see and hear. They will bring back rocks and houses, cars and wind, even roses and violets. And they will bring back stars colliding with planets, the little spots people forgot to paint, a grasshopper that looks like a heart with legs. Even the rusted gray fence will turn the color of a dolphin. Tomorrow we will break ground and plant.

Yiskah Rosenfeld
San Francisco Community School

why i teach writing

(for karleen)

>she showed up
>every saturday
>backpack bursting with papers
>to tell us
>words didn't belong
>to schoolbooks to social workers
>to shakespeare to the president
>to tell us
>words belonged to us
>
>she gave us
>>the alphabet like a soft old blanket
>>letters like bullets
>>names for our desires
>
>she gave us
>the keys to her apartment
>so we could use her computer
>met us in cafes and taquerias
>just to talk
>she brought the college catalog
>and sat with us on her back steps
>choosing classes
>
>she gave me
>the first poem i ever understood
>the first book i read with
>characters like me
>the concept
>hope
>
>she told me to write
>and i wrote
>and writing gave me back
>the kid with skinned knees
>and home-sewn clothes
>who raced boys around the block
>and won
>the girl who swore
>and screamed at teachers

who fired rocks from a slingshot
with perfect aim

i wrote
and started thinking less
about how to kill myself
and more about what i wanted to be
when i grew up

i wrote
and i stopped keeping razors
in the hems of my clothes
in case i got locked up again
i wrote and the scars on my arms faded
and my poems became birds
that could fly back through the barbed wire
the bulletproof glass
the concrete walls
into the asylum and sing
comfort to the kids inside

so now i show up
with my satchel full
of crumpled photocopies
to say:
words don't belong
to the police
to the prosecutor
to judges   or professors   or senators
not to experts, doctors, millionaires
not to mtv   not to abc
not to sony
or time
or hearst corporation.

words
    belong
        to all of us.

                Danielle Montgomery
                Center for Young Women's Development
                Ida B. Wells High School

Whatever Gets You Through the Night
or
Hot Manju

[LEE, an Asian American youth, stands in front of his fellow juvenile rehabilitation ranch residents. It is his last day at the ranch and he is being asked to give some words about how he got through his program. A program is the number of months a youth has been assigned by the court for the crime he committed.]

                LEE
What got me through the nights?
    [Beat.]
One. My parents disowning me. Especially my mom. My dad disowned me years ago. But my mom, that's a different story. If she disowns me…I'm alone. You know: *alone*.
    [Beat.]
Two. Hot manju. You probably never had the pleasure, but if you haven't tried these baked babies straight out of the oven when the crust's light and flaky, the inside's soft and melty, well…you haven't lived. All I think about is when I get out, first thing I'm going to do is have hot manju. It's what got me through that time when a certain resident offered me a joint in the laundry room and I passed. Or that time when a certain someone else said, "Man, let's take it out of bounds or I'll pull a pistol on ya when we're on the outs," and I didn't say a word. Any time you're going to lose it, think: *hot manju*.
    [Beat.]
One last thing…To all you haters out there, and you know who you are, I understand now. I understand why you crabs try to pull down the ones doin' good on our program. I understand why you said, "Hey, Lee, got more of that good stuff?" when a counselor walked by, and got me thirty more days on my program. I mean, why should *any* of us give a damn? What reason do *we* have to get up in the morning and say, "Gee whiz, just going to change my life today!" Let's be real. We're the front line. Shock troops of a drug war. First to get shot

up, first to get locked up. You could say, "Man, I don't give a you-know-what, so before this life ends, I'm going to mess up as many people as I can." I wouldn't blame you, but think about that for a moment. There are millions of kids all walking around with that same "f— it" attitude, like robots ready to self-destruct. You think *you* benefit from that? When kids kill each other 'cause they're from a different gang, race, whatever, the only person who benefits is the guy not even there. The guy who lives 'cross town in a nice pretty house and reads the next morning's headlines: "More Kids Die over Stupid Reasons," turns to his wife and says, "Oh well." *You* want to help *them*? Why not do something to show them who you *really* are? Check this out: You're on the outs and you go enjoy your new freedom down at Union Square when some yuppie white girl gives you that *look*. You know the one: Grabs purse tight, fear of God in the face. And then you go up to her, stare straight into those shaking eyes and say, "Hey, you…Yeah, you…I read your mind, girl. And you know what? I'm working some more magic on you. I'm turning your mind *inside out*. 'Cause I got more smarts, creativity, insight, beauty, power than you could *ever* hold in that little Gucci purse of yours. And by the way…Have a great day." And after you got that off your chest, go down to J-town. Take the Geary bus to this bakery in the mall and order yourself the best plate of hot manju you never had. Trust me. You won't regret it.

    [LEE smiles and leaves.]

Peter Tamaribuchi
Log Cabin Ranch

Mission Girls

Dedicated to Karla Castillo and all the hard-working mujeres at YWCA Mission Girls Services.

I. Las Niñas

in the middle
of a writing exercise
Josselyn asks me
how to spell
birthday
i tell her

it doesn't matter
we'll check spelling later

how to spell
invitation

put your ideas down first

my name?

she hands me
the green index card—
i'm officially invited
to her eighth birthday party
on a Saturday in April

today is a Tuesday in January
i wonder what her mother
will say to seating
a 35-year-old guest.

II. Las Jovenes

The first few sessions,
Veronica stares at me blankly.
Eventually she relaxes enough
to grimace when I look her way.
When I try to melt her with a joke,

she counters with,
"That's not funny, Cathy."
We both laugh.

She hid in the bathroom
with Aurita two summers ago,
locked themselves in
while Karla, the other girls,
their families, and I waited,
wondering if they would finish
the poetry reading or not.
Not.

Two weeks ago,
they each read a poem
for International Women's Month
at the Mission Cultural Center.

III. Las Señoritas

Many attend community college,
some ask for help
with the classes that give grades.
Silvia and I spend many hours
spread over a few weeks
on an essay
for her English class.

Two weeks later,
she shows me the B.
I see the proud smile
on her face.

IV. Mi Niñez

Growing up in the '70s and '80s,
my Mission girls
were my sister
and five girl cousins.

When I started to write
my first story,
I was eight or nine.
I stopped.

Stories were not about
young colored girls
who lived with cousins,
aunts, uncles,
and grandparents
on streets named Guerrero.

I erased my family
my street
my city
my self.

These days,
when I pass out
Tweety-bird pencils
or smooth blue pens,
I hope to fill in
the erasure.
I want to help
leave a mark.

Cathy Arellano
YWCA Mission Girls Services
Mission High School
Loco Bloco

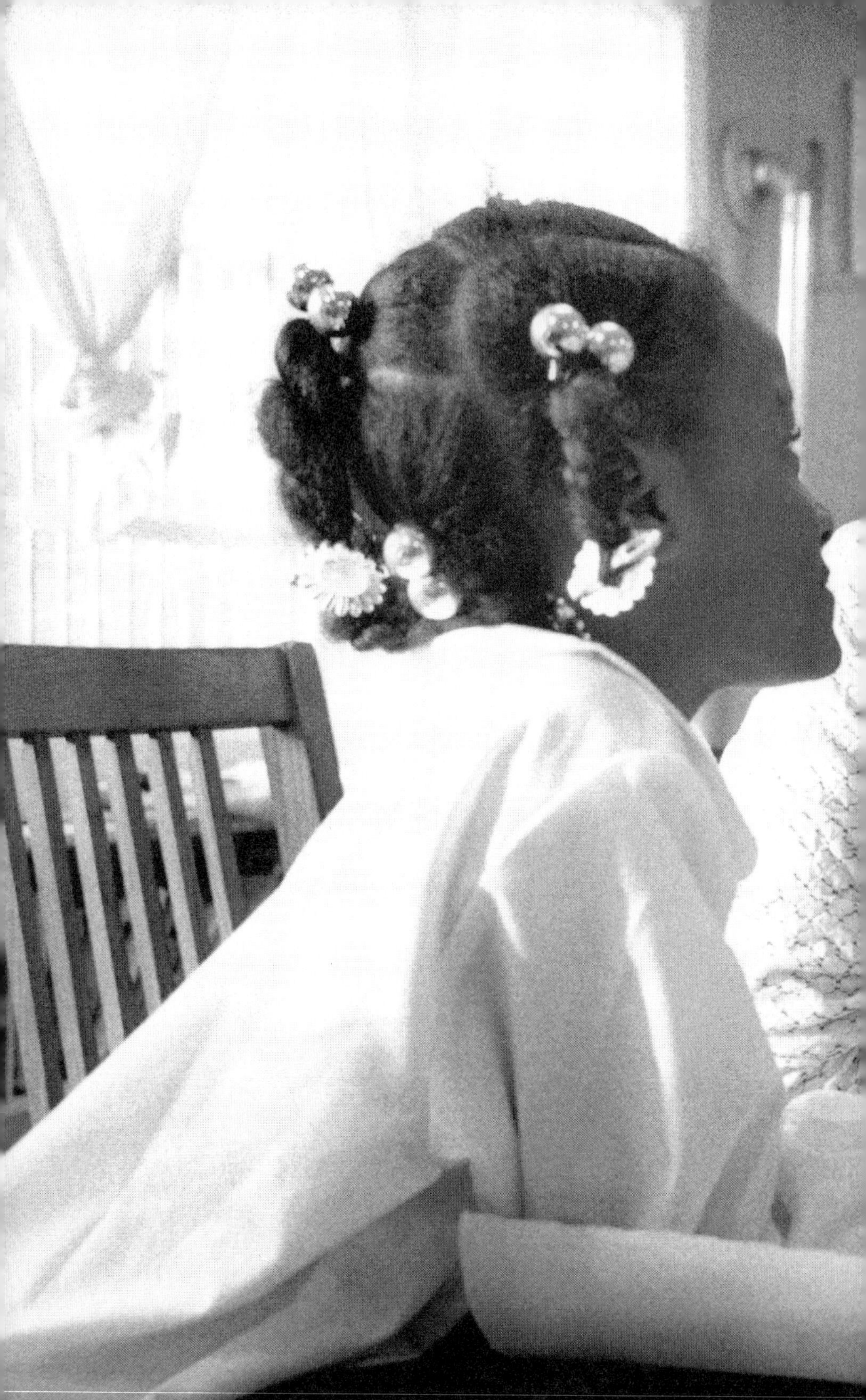

Girls After School Academy

Trying to Be Men

I hear them.
DeAngelo, Edward, Octavio, Cleveland,
Eric, Wesley, David, Jamar.
Lines of their poems run
like ticker tape through my mind.
Uncanny literary visitations while
I grocery shop or swim.

As I drive home from Log Cabin Ranch I remember Robert
escaped over that ridge with the help of a full moon.
But I know when they run they never get far enough away.
I hear Nate's hoarse "I love you," as great gusts of wind blow
sand over the highway near Pescadero.
He was sick of hating.

In the Mission I see Sammy, or his twin,
or Anthony, Tommy, Angelo, Ernesto.
We say hello, how you doin'—
where we couldn't speak otherwise,
our eyes wouldn't meet if not for my job.

By my desk photos of the big events:
Marvin reading at the Civic,
David, Onnie, Eric, Terrell,
on the mike at the library podium.
The beaming Slam teams:
Daniel, Marcus, John, Andrew, Sean,
Damyan, Charles, Raymond, Scott, Oliver,
Kethan, Anthony, Djalma, Sammy.

They people my life, clown in my memory
knock at my breastbone with loss,
love, and relentless histrionic style.
I repeat their stories and wonder
where they are now, send off
quick urgent prayers. There are so many.

I have new students, I need to let the others go, trust
they will find their lives. We have printed each other with words.

But I don't trust their future with its menacing litany
of problems and violent rules of survival.

I cannot let them go peacefully
into the fluorescent prisons that await them. I hold on,
crowded with handshakes and penciled addresses, photos
and file cabinets of carefully scribbled poems, voices
still in my ear, teaching me all the ways they try
to be men, learning money before love,
making grave mistakes.

I hold on,
and I will not forget.

                                        Kimberley Nelson
                                        Log Cabin Ranch

The Arc of Intention

I.

Lotus
flowers reflected in a pond,
students bend

their necks
over the shallow surface of
paper, fixing

the light of their divine
gaze
inward

where the pencil is a scorpion,
storm cloud,
grove of swaying orange trees.

II.

Again, the arc
is in them,
overwhelming, precise.
They gather at high windows,
stretch on tiptoe, lean out
to see better, the rooftops, antennae,
ships on the bay—to name
this world with the jagged
awkward words, the borrowed

words—yet they are naming!
And through the windows the city
rises to meet them: *cable* and *goldfinch*,
plum blossom and *crane*,
water tower, *cypress*. They try on the new

syllables like foreign hats, over-
sized robes, some soldier's
lost boot. In this way, the words
are tamed, even loved, and their faces

wear the glow, unmistakably,
of the sublime,
the gull's slow circling
reflected in church windows
or ghostly *cirrus clouds*
wandering pine mountains, unseen,
until now—the Word!
They delight here, emergent,
shiny as found medallions,

their families' lost heirlooms
worn all the while round their necks
invisibly—the Word!
The way
space contemplates
itself, the way bamboo leans
over its ravine, hangs there, balanced
along its curve
into gravity. Everything

is shaped by that
leaning: *love* and
resistance, the rapt
arc
of intention.
The five-year-old has it, even,
with her blue
crayon, writing and rewriting her
name! Her name!

                        Chad Sweeney
                        Everett Middle School
                        Mercy Services

Libation for the Present and Future

Visualize
Visualize
Visualize
Visualize

Visualize the arrival of Peace.

Its weave and weight, how as it unfolds
it warms the hearts
of those who hold it from deep within.
Visualize the arrival of Peace.

Visualize a positive Peace,

unafraid to speak her mind
unafraid to hear another person's spoken
unafraid to embrace dissent.
Visualize a positive Peace.

Visualize an unwavering peace.

Peace does not yield, but stands his ground
and yet isn't afraid to lay the guns down.
Peace isn't afraid to lay the guns down.
Visualize an unwavering peace.

Visualize an enduring peace,

passed on to future generations
untarnished by inevitable confrontations
revitalized by constant reaffirmations.
Visualize an enduring Peace.

Visualize the arrival of Peace
Visualize a positive Peace
Visualize an unwavering Peace
Visualize an enduring Peace

Visualize
Visualize
Visualize
Visualize

Gloria Yamato
Girls After School Academy
Ida B. Wells High School

Make Room

The old choir room until the roof began to leak,
the room with the piano until it was filled with boxes of books,
the small library room until the computers needed storing,
room 222 when the math tutor isn't there
        but not sixth period Thursdays because of Boys Group,
Mr. Z's room fifth period because the sixth graders have lunch,
Ms. A's room sixth period prep but don't erase anything
        on the chalkboard,
306 but not during eighth period because of Reading,
the library when there are no classes checking out books.

This is how it is to be a writer,
I tell them
as we walk down the hallway,
backpacks heavy on our shoulders,
looking for an empty place,
a home
we build with words.

Michelle Matz
Everett Middle School

The text of this book was set in Electra, designed for Mergenthaler by W.A. Dwiggins in 1935. Display type is Trade Gothic, also designed for Mergenthaler by Jackson Burke in 1948. The interior and cover were printed on Fox River Coronado white smooth in 80 lb. text and cover weights accordingly. The book was printed by Somerset Printing in Burlingame, California, using match ink colors and black. Photographs by Ed Kashi were scanned from original prints. Book design and typography were executed by Thomas Ingalls and Sara Streifel of Ingalls + Associates of San Francisco.

SEP 6 '02